Contents

Chapter 1: Consumer trends

Mintel reveals UK consumer trends of 2014	1
Four hours, one cup of posh coffee and £117.32 spent – the perfect shopping trip	4
Online retailing: Britain, Europe and the US 2014	5
E-commerce turns 20 and my, how it's grown	7
Four in ten consumers influenced by social media when researching products	8
The science that makes us spend more in supermarkets, and feel good while we do it	9
Same-day delivery a new threat to retailers	11
The tricky business of advertising to children	12
Food giants target children with addictive 'advergames'	14
Branded for life? Researchers examine impact of consumer culture on UK's children	15
BrandIndex rankings 2013	16

Chapter 2: Consumer rights

Consumer contracts regulations	17
Accepting returns and giving refunds: the law	20
Online and distance selling for businesses	21
Key facts on the new EU Consumer Rights Directive	22
What are my rights when buying digital content?	23
Protect yourself	24
Should Sunday trading restrictions be relaxed?	26

Chapter 3: Ethics & developments

Public views on ethical retail	28
Ethical Consumer Markets Report 2013	30
To what degree do ethics play a role in consumers' purchasing decisions?	31
How much do consumers really care about transparency?	32
Top five ethical shopping tips	34
The future of shopping: from high street to iStreet	35
Future of British high streets will see fewer retailers, more services and better community activities	37
Hard to please 'fauxsumers' pin it and save it but rarely buy it	39

Key facts	40
Glossary	41
Assignments	42
Index	43
Acknowledgements	44

Introduction

Consumerism is Volume 276 in the **ISSUES** series. The aim of the series is to offer current, diverse information about important issues in our world, from a UK perspective.

ABOUT CONSUMERISM

Since the advent of e-commerce, consumerism has evolved exponentially. In 2013, online retailing in Europe grew to £111.2 billion with online retail sales via mobile devices expected to grow to £7.62 billion. The high street, however, is suffering, with 27% of stores in the UK sitting vacant in January 2014. This book explores the development of e-commerce and the future of shopping. It also examines your rights as a consumer and considers the role of ethical consumerism in today's society.

OUR SOURCES

Titles in the **ISSUES** series are designed to function as educational resource books, providing a balanced overview of a specific subject.

The information in our books is comprised of facts, articles and opinions from many different sources, including:

⇨ Newspaper reports and opinion pieces

⇨ Website factsheets

⇨ Magazine and journal articles

⇨ Statistics and surveys

⇨ Government reports

⇨ Literature from special interest groups.

A NOTE ON CRITICAL EVALUATION

Because the information reprinted here is from a number of different sources, readers should bear in mind the origin of the text and whether the source is likely to have a particular bias when presenting information (or when conducting their research). It is hoped that, as you read about the many aspects of the issues explored in this book, you will critically evaluate the information presented.

It is important that you decide whether you are being presented with facts or opinions. Does the writer give a biased or unbiased report? If an opinion is being expressed, do you agree with the writer? Is there potential bias to the 'facts' or statistics behind an article?

ASSIGNMENTS

In the back of this book, you will find a selection of assignments designed to help you engage with the articles you have been reading and to explore your own opinions. Some tasks will take longer than others and there is a mixture of design, writing and research-based activities that you can complete alone or in a group.

FURTHER RESEARCH

At the end of each article we have listed its source and a website that you can visit if you would like to conduct your own research. Please remember to critically evaluate any sources that you consult and consider whether the information you are viewing is accurate and unbiased.

Useful weblinks

www.72point.com

www.bostonglobe.com

www.brandindex.com

www.theconversation.com

discuss.bis.gov.uk

ec.europa.eu European Commission

www.ethicalconsumer.org

www.fca.org.uk Financial Conduct Authority

www.internetretailing.net

www.mintel.com

www.performancein.com

www.retailresearch.org

www.retail-week.com

www.sussex.ac.uk

www.which.co.uk

Gower College Swansea

Gorseinon : Swansea : SA4 6RD Tel: (01792) 890731
This resource is **YOUR RESPONSIBILITY** and is due for
return/renewal on or before the last date shown.

CLASS NO. 658·324 ACR   ACC. NO. GCS046399

RETURN OR RENEW - DON'T PAY FINES

Independence Educational Publishers

First published by Independence Educational Publishers

The Studio, High Green

Great Shelford

Cambridge CB22 5EG

England

© Independence 2015

Photocopy licence

The material in this book is protected by copyright. However, the
purchaser is free to make multiple copies of particular articles for instructional
purposes for immediate use within the purchasing institution.
Making copies of the entire book is not permitted.

British Library Cataloguing in Publication Data

Consumerism. -- (Issues ; 276)

1. Consumption (Economics) 2. Electronic commerce.

3. Consumer behavior.

I. Series II. Acred, Cara editor.

381.3-dc23

ISBN-13: 9781861687043

Printed in Great Britain

Zenith Print Group

Mintel reveals UK consumer trends for 2014

Mintel's Senior Trends Consultant Richard Cope outlines the four trends set to impact the consumer market in the UK, examining the areas of commercial opportunity for brands – and what consumers will be buying into in 2014.

1 – Internationalism on the agenda

'After a period of Brand Britannia fever, driven by Olympic medals, Royal weddings and births, in 2014 it will be time for British consumers to look outwards at other countries. Next year's sporting events, immigration legislation and pending referendums will put other countries' products on the menu and Mintel's research highlights that Brits are open, curious and savvy when it comes to buying into new,

engaging or better value products from abroad.'

'Mintel's research finds that in spite of recent events, "patriotic purchasing" remains something of a myth and British custom is there to be won: 48% of consumers agree that "price matters more than whether a product is British" and 30% say "I do not feel any loyalty to buying British food and drink". Further Mintel research reveals that price comes before patriotism and provenance with 58% of consumers saying "the price and the quality of what I buy is what matters, not where it was produced". Meanwhile, 54% of Brits say that they're "just as interested in buying authentic products (e.g. French Brie, Parma ham) from other countries as from Britain".'

'In 2014, a number of factors will focus consumers' attention on

the provenance of products from inside and outside the UK. The FIFA World Cup and Winter Olympics will see British consumers fed a diet of Brazilian and Russian products and campaigns, whilst the Commonwealth Games will become an early rallying point for the run-up to Scottish independence referendum. Whilst this means that the very concept of the United Kingdom is up for review, Scottish products and provenance will enjoy a heightened profile.'

'New legislation in 2014 will also raise the foreign influx and influence in the UK, piquing our curiosity in other cultures and causing us to re-examine notions of "Britishness". The Government is simplifying its visa processes for admitting Chinese visitors to the EU and in January 2014, temporary migration and employment restrictions on citizens of Romania and Bulgaria will be lifted in the UK. Mintel's research highlights that the British are largely tolerant and open to embracing new cultural influences. Indeed, 74% of consumers say "Tolerance of others is an important part of British culture" and 50% agree with the statement that "Being British is now as much about embracing different cultures as it is about sticking to British traditions", compared with 20% who disagree. This is borne out by further Mintel research – where just 8% of diners have visited a Polish restaurant but 42% are interested in doing so and an impressive 12% of the UK population say that they celebrate Hanukkah, Ramadan or Diwali.'

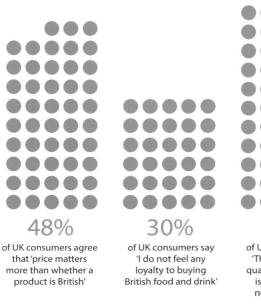

48%
of UK consumers agree that 'price matters more than whether a product is British'

30%
of UK consumers say 'I do not feel any loyalty to buying British food and drink'

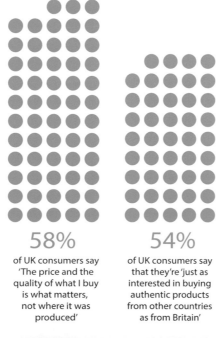

58%
of UK consumers say 'The price and the quality of what I buy is what matters, not where it was produced'

54%
of UK consumers say that they're 'just as interested in buying authentic products from other countries as from Britain'

2 – Club Tropicalia

'The World Cup is going to make the world fall in love with all things Brazilian. The country's place in the cultural and commercial spotlight has been a long time coming: it has not hosted a World Cup since 1950 and it's almost as long since the 1950s Bossa Nova and 1960s Tropicalia movements brought its music to a global audience. This time around the showcase of Brazilian commercial cultural exports will encompass everything from food to fashion to beauty products.'

'The Olympic handover ceremony at the close of London 2012 showcased the talents of singers Marisa Monte and Seu Jorge, but probably confounded and engaged UK viewers in the same tantalising fashion that the opening ceremony did for the rest of the world. There is no doubt about the fact that billions will be watching back home and this creates enormous potential for British consumers to be exposed to and buy into all manner of Brazilian products and services. Brazilian brands are alive to the opportunity, with trade association Wines of Brazil aiming to double exports between 2012 and 2016. Meanwhile, It may be news to foreign consumers, but Moët et Chandon has been producing a Chandon Brazilian sparkling wine in the Bento Gonçalves area of Southern Brazil since the 1970s and the country is an emerging wine producer with the potential to crossover to a wider market.'

'When it comes to food and drink, UK consumers are open to new tastes from around the world, as some 50% of wine, 42% of beer and 40% of spirit drinkers agree with the statement "I like to try drinks from different countries". It's early days on the product launches front, but Brazilian UK product launches include Brazilian Pão de Queijo – or Cheese Bread – Mix, Antarctica's Guaraná soft drink and Brazil's national beer Brahma. As an accompaniment to watching football, Cachaça has enormous potential, with Velho Barreiro and Sagatiba the brands to look out for – and with Mintel research showing that the market in Brazil is in decline as consumers there trade up to imported alcohol, there is also a strong export opportunity. In addition, the caipirinha cocktail now comes in many guises with Cachaça substituted by vodka (a caipiroska) and rum (a caipirissima). Brazilians are also passionate about meat and churrasco chain restaurants like Rodízio Rico, Rodízio Preto and Braza have the potential to appeal to those 60% of UK consumers who have not but would like to visit a South American restaurant. There's also potential for Açaí berries – eaten as both an exercise fuel and relaxing snack in Brazil – as well as Brazilian branded coconut water products.'

'In fashion, brands such as Havaianas are already well known in the UK, especially as 51% of shoe shoppers agree that well-known branded footwear is worth paying more for – but other leading Brazilian beachwear brands including Água de Coco, Salinas and Blue Man have potential. Beauty is perhaps the segment where Brazil is most established in the consciousness of British consumers, but there is potential for more products, services and brands to cross over. Mintel's research shows that 18% of haircare users are interested and willing to pay more for products which provide temporary straightening or smoothing benefits. On the "beach chic" front, the Sol de Janeiro suncare line is positioned as "reflecting the beauty and purity of a Brazilian beach experience". According to Mintel's research, 12% of those interested in using self-tanning products don't use a high SPF because they want a tan and 39% use or would use self-tanning products to give them a holiday glow, meaning that Brazilian products have the potential to capture the summer market.'

3 – A private function

'With the launch of Google Glass and the fallout from the NSA revelations, surveillance and data monitoring will continue to be big news in 2014. We're going to see consumers looking for greater privacy – but also greater functionality – from their data as they bid to take further control of it to help them to streamline their lives and better analyse themselves. All of this is raising discussion around data privacy, but also its value and usability.'

'Mintel's research shows that intrusion and privacy are indeed issues for brands to heed; indeed, 23% of consumers say they "find video adverts that target you according to your Internet activity off-putting", whilst 59% of consumers agree that online advertising that is based on their browsing history makes them feel uncomfortable and 19% are concerned about how aggregators use personal data. Yet consumers are embracing self-analysis, with 9% of health-conscious consumers having used online health trackers to help them stay on track. Beyond the cutting-edge areas such as wearable tech, the greatest opportunity for self-analysis could lie in the humble

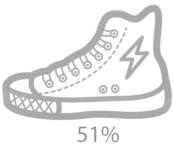

51%
of UK shoe shoppers agree that well-known branded footwear is worth paying more for

39%
of UK consumers interested in using self-tanning products would use them for a holiday glow

loyalty card – something that 66% of UK consumers use according to Mintel's research.'

'The next stage is for grocery brands to offer positive data surveillance for customers – in the form of opt-in nutritional analysis services. Mintel's research shows that the will is there amongst consumers: 17% of consumers say they like the idea of information on their receipt informing them how healthy their shopping basket is, whilst 36% of UK grocery shoppers say they would be interested in a nutritional review of basket content.'

'In 2014 we can expect the commercial launch of Google Glass alongside Google Glass App Store, but the imminent launch of a Google Smartwatch might be earlier – and bigger – news. One reason that wearable technology may be warmly welcomed is its ability to track the location of loved ones – something increasingly important in an era of working "Alpha Mothers" and multi-generational homes that care for elderly relatives. We've already seen the launch of the FiLIP – a wrist device for kids that acts as both a smartphone and a locator for worried parents – and similar technology can take off for all ages.'

4 – Healthy fuels

'In the coming year we will see consumers moving away from caffeine and further towards functional green vegetable drinks. In late 2014 new EU food and drink labelling legislation (the Food Information Regulation) will extend beyond the current situation, where drinks containing more than 150mg of caffeine per litre (mg/l) are deemed to have "high caffeine content", to "require additional caffeine labelling for high-caffeine drinks and foods where caffeine is added for a physiological effect". This is going to place pressure on the energy drinks brands and in the run-up to this legislation we're going to see a new wave of competition from natural and vegetable drinks launches.'

'According to Mintel's research, UK consumers would appear very open to the prospect of new "healthy' launches within the energy drinks sector. Indeed, some 38% of UK consumers agree that "fruit and vegetable juice blends are healthier for you than pure fruit juice". At Mintel we've already seen a host of global new launches in late 2013, including the launch of Coca-Cola life in Argentina (2204268), a low-calorie carbonated drink "naturally sweetened with Truvia" – packaged in green as a distinctive move away from red. Indeed, in the UK alone new product launches of drinks with a no additives or preservatives claim grew 56% over the past five years to 2012. Meanwhile, new UK drinks product launches with a low/no/reduced sugar claim increased 63% over the same period.'

'In 2014 we're going to see a lot of launch activity from brands in a bid to react early to this pending legislation. The big opportunity here is that both non-users and users of the current energy drinks brands appear ready to try a new alternative: Mintel's research shows 34% of energy drinks users claim they "worry about becoming reliant on them for an energy boost", whilst 37% of non-users cited the fact that "they contain too many artificial ingredients or colourants". In contrast, there appears to be a bright future for energy drinks with a natural, functional dimension, with 72% of consumers saying that "there should be healthier (e.g. sugar/calorie-free) varieties", 71% that "there should be more drinks with natural colourings/flavourings" and 41% that "It's worth paying more for added benefits (e.g. added vitamins)".'

18 November 2013

⇨ The above information is reprinted with kind permission from Mintel. Please visit www.mintel.com for further information.

© Mintel 2014

Four hours, one cup of posh coffee and £117.32 spent – the perfect shopping trip

The perfect shopping trip involves a four-hour trawl around stores, one cup of posh coffee and a cake – and a modest £117.32 dent in the bank balance, it has been revealed. Researchers, who polled 2,000 women who are regular shoppers, also found the ideal expedition to the local shopping centre would include a 25-minute journey leading to the purchase of seven items.

Finding something you've wanted for ages in a sale and discovering you can comfortably fit into a garment one size smaller than you usually wear are also essential.

Vouchers and gift cards to spend to the tune of £60 and not having to queue for longer than six minutes also make a shopping trip idyllic for women.

The study shows women like to shop on the high street fortnightly, preferably alone rather than in the company of friends.

A spokesman for Gift Card & Voucher Week, which commissioned the research, said:

The simple fact of the matter is that women absolutely love shopping, and so are happy to traipse around high street stores and shopping centres at least once every two weeks.

'But a successful shopping trip isn't just about browsing for hours on end, it's about getting to spend a decent amount of money, going back home armed with several shopping bags and a new wardrobe of clothes.

'And eight out of ten women said they would rather receive a gift card or vouchers than someone choosing a gift for them – this would make things absolutely perfect.

'The absolutely idyllic trip is one which is full of surprises – bargains, sales, clothes which fit first time, shorter queues, helpful shop assistants and stacks of money to spend.'

Researchers found the average woman is quite happy to browse her way around seven different shops, revisiting at least two to make up her mind.

Favourite shops are clothing, shoes and beauty, and although girls like to shop alone they'll phone or text at least two friends to discuss their purchases.

In contrast, the survey found the average man only embarks on three shopping trips across the entire year.

Rather than visiting the shops frequently, men prefer shopping online, and as such are only prepared to go every four months.

But when they do go, they'd rather go in the company of their other half than on their own but only want to hit the shops for a maximum of one hour and 45 minutes.

On each occasion they'll spend around £200 on goods, and rarely bother trying anything on before they buy.

Favourite shops are any which sell electrical or technical products, or gadgets.

A fifth of men are happier if they can stop to check the football scores, while others just need a few minutes to recover from the experience with a pint or coffee.

But both men and women agree that a shopping trip is far from perfect unless they can stop in the pub afterwards for at least three drinks.

Interestingly, women will spend a whopping £3,050.32 on high street shopping trips across the course of one year, compared to spends of just £611.43 for men.

The spokeswoman for Gift Card & Voucher Week added:

'Men really are a different breed of creature to women.

'When it comes to shopping, it's a needs must affair. It is not an event in the calendar which men look forward to, or indeed want to do.

'This is why the shopping trip is shorter, and to the point. There is no messing around with trying clothes on, revisiting shops or browsing.

'Men tend to walk into a shop, choose what they want, buy it, and leave.'

Average shopping trip for women:

⇨ Shop for four hours

⇨ One coffee/lunch break mid shopping trip

⇨ Browse seven clothes shops

⇨ Try on all clothing before buying

⇨ Revisit at least two shops

⇨ Buy a minimum of seven items

⇨ Preferred shops are clothes, shoes, health and beauty

⇨ Spend £117.32

⇨ Gift cards and vouchers worth £60 to spend

⇨ Talk/discuss purchases with at least 3 shopping assistants

⇨ Shop alone

⇨ Phone/text two friends while shopping

⇨ Embark on a 25-minute journey to the shops

⇨ Happy to queue for six minutes

⇨ Expect to carry at least four bags home

- ⇨ Love the first thing you try on
- ⇨ Something you want for ages is in the sale
- ⇨ You are a dress size smaller than you thought you were
- ⇨ 26% end the trip with a visit to the pub for three drinks
- ⇨ Prefers high street shopping

Go on two shopping trips a month

Average shopping trip for men:

- ⇨ Shop for one hour and 45 minutes
- ⇨ One break mid shopping trip for a pint or coffee
- ⇨ Buy clothes without trying anything on
- ⇨ Browse three clothes shops
- ⇨ Buy a maximum of six items
- ⇨ Preferred shops are electrical/technical and gadget stores
- ⇨ Spend £203.81
- ⇨ Gift cards and vouchers worth £52 to spend
- ⇨ Talk/discuss purchases with at least three shopping assistants
- ⇨ Phone/text two friends while shopping
- ⇨ Prefer to shop with a partner
- ⇨ Prepared to travel for 25 minutes to the shops
- ⇨ Happy to queue for six minutes
- ⇨ Expect to carry at least four bags home
- ⇨ A third of men end the trip with a visit to the pub for three drinks
- ⇨ A fifth like to have time to stop and check the football scores
- ⇨ Prefers online shopping

Go on three shopping trips a year

11 November 2013

- ⇨ The above information is reprinted with kind permission from 72 point. Please visit www.72point.com for further information.

Online retailing: Britain, Europe and the US 2014

E-commerce is the fastest growing retail market in Europe, with sales in the UK, Germany, France, Sweden, The Netherlands, Italy, Poland and Spain expected to reach a combined total of £111.2 billion in 2014 (€155.3 billion or $212.8 billion). We expect online sales in the US to reach $306.0 billion (€224.0 billion) in 2014.

Our independent study for 2014–15 has been funded by RetailMeNot, Inc., the world's largest digital coupon marketplace (known in the UK as MyCoupon.com) as a contribution to discussion.

Areas studied

The Centre for Retail Research has estimated the trends in online retail sales for eight European countries (see above) and the US. This is based on the sales of goods (excluding fuel for vehicles and sales of prepared food in cafes and restaurants). Tickets, holidays, gambling and insurance are also excluded because they are not classed as retailing. 'Online' is defined as sales where the final transaction is made over the Internet or at a distance, irrespective of whether the Internet has been used for browsing and price comparisons. Sales made using mobile phones and tablets are included in our figures.

1,000 shoppers in each country (a representative demographic cross section) have been surveyed for this project and 100 online traders in each country. We have taken advantage of new data to produce results that are more accurate overall.

Main results: onwards and upwards

In 2013, online retailing in Europe grew by a weighted average of 21.1% to £111.2 billion, but growth should slacken slightly in 2014 to 18.1%. The recession has induced many shoppers to buy online rather from traditional stores, whilst above-average growth in countries with smaller e-commerce sectors shows there has been an element of catch up. Retail focus on

the growing use of mobile technology is an additional factor in making online retailing attractive and convenient.

As before, the European online market is dominated by the UK, Germany and France which together are responsible for 81.3% of European sales in these eight countries.

Market shares

Apart from the UK and Germany, market shares are low in most European countries. The weighted average in 2014 is expected to be 7.2% (6.3% in 2013).

The UK online share of retailing is expected to rise from 12.1% (2013) to 13.5% (2014). The German online sector has expanded rapidly in 2012–13 but we expect the rate of increase to decline but its market share will still rise to 9.7% in 2014.

Over the next four years we expect the major players to continue to expand (at a lower growth rate than hitherto) and the smaller online countries to grow quickly thus reducing the discrepancies between different states.

US online spending 2013–14

US online spending was $268 billion in 2013 and we forecast it will reach $306 billion in 2014, an increase of 14.5%. If we use the same definition of retail sales that is used in Europe then the US share of retail (i.e. sales of goods) in 2013 was 10.6% and is estimated to reach 11.6% in 2014. There has been a lot of discussion in the US about when the online share would break through the 10% barrier (and we have contributed to that) but this has already been achieved if one eliminates the broader non-retail merchandise from the US definition of the retail industry as is already done in Europe.

The US is still the leader in online retailing compared to Europe. With a similar population to the eight countries surveyed, 54.5% of the US public were eshoppers compared to 45.6% in Europe. Every online shopper in Europe is expected to spend €886.18 (£748.82 or $1,210.63) in 2014 compared to €1,308.29 (£1,105.51 or $1,787.28) in the US.

Mobile shopping

Online orders made using mobile technology (smartphones and tablets) in 2013 were 8.0% of all online sales in Europe but as high as 13.8% in the US. The percentages for browsing were much higher but these totals refer to the final transaction (ordering and paying) not the entire process, where between one-third and 45% of retail website visits may be done on mobiles.

In 2014 we expect online retail sales made via mobiles to grow in the UK by 62% to a total of £7.92 billion. This is equivalent to 17.6% of UK online retail sales. Sales using tablets will grow by 100% (to £3.10 billion) and smartphone retailing is expected to grow by 44.3% to £4.82 billion. Smartphones will still provide 60.8% of UK mobile shopping. Other European countries with high mobile shares will be Germany (16.8% of German online sales [£5.59 billion or €6.61 billion] and Sweden (16.5% of Swedish online retail sales [£0.59 billion or €0.70 billion]). French mobile spending is expected to be 13.5% of online retail sales in 2014 (£3.56 billion or €4.21 billion).

Mobile shopping will represent 13.1% of the online retail spend in 2014 or £19.78 billion.

In the US, mobile shopping is growing even faster and should grow by 65.1% to account for 19.9% of online spending in 2014 (£37.66 billion or $61.06 billion). Of this 40.0% will be tablet sales and 60.0% on smartphones.

Effect on traditional stores

The growth of online sales at such a rate will inevitably reduce the market for traditional shops. By the time that online sales represent 5% or more of domestic retailing then the continued growth of online retailers will occur at the expense of conventional stores. In Europe as a whole, online retailers are expanding 11.9 times faster than conventional outlets, although 'only' 5.6 times in the UK and 3.3 times in the US.

Stages in market development

We think there are three stages in online market development and business strategy:

Maturity – market share of 9.5% or above, 55%+ of the population are Internet shoppers, rapidly developing mobile use (15%+ of all online in 2014), multiple online providers throughout each sector and 12+ purchases p.a. by each shopper.

Mid range – market shares of 6.5% to 9.5%, a wide range of suppliers, more than ten purchases p.a. per shopper, 45% are online shoppers and a smaller mobile use.

Immature – online market share below 6.5%, patchy takeup (regionally or demographically) of online retailing, fewer than ten purchases pa, and some trade sectors are comparatively less developed.

Mature markets, such as the US, the UK and Germany, are expected to grow more slowly, recruiting a percentage of non-users but mainly growing because existing eshoppers place more orders or buy more expensive items.

Mid-range markets, such as France, The Netherlands and Sweden, will grow by recruiting more users as well as persuading shoppers to buy more frequently.

Immature markets, such as Italy, Spain and Poland, have to overcome structural issues in the quality of their telecommunication networks, but can be expected to develop rapidly by increasing the number of eshoppers in their population and then inducing them to purchase more regularly.

Are the statistics right?

Methods

The statistics are problematic as state statistical research organisations often tend to underestimate the size of the sector, because conventionally they are best at collecting information from companies that own retail shops. There can be problems in determining online sales from abroad, because UK statistical authorities may not be fully aware of their scale, foreign firms may not wish to comply fully with UK statistical needs, and sampling may be problematic as a result of rapid sector change. There are important issues about whether to include mail order when it is mainly online and how to account for partial online ordering such as click and collect. Other issues include the definition of 'retail' where US authorities seem to combine food services (cafes and restaurants) within retail, which is not the case in Europe. However, in Europe and the US, fuel for cars is normally included as 'retail' but as this is not the retailing of goods and would be difficult to sell over the web we have attempted to adjust our estimates to take account of this.

⇨ The above information is reprinted with kind permission from the Centre for Retail Research. Please visit www.retailresearch. org for further information.

© Centre for Retail Research 2014

Online retail sales	Online sales (£ billion) 2013	Growth 2013	Online Sales (£ billion) 2014	Growth 2014
UK	£38.83	16.8%	£44.97	15.8%
Germany	£28.98	39.2%	£35.36	22.0%
France	£22.65	12.0%	£26.38	16.5%
Spain	£5.75	22.5%	£6.87	19.6%
Italy	£4.48	18.6%	£5.33	19.0%
Netherlands	£4.48	11.6%	£5.09	13.5%
Sweden	£3.13	15.9%	£3.61	15.5%
Poland	£2.92	24.0%	£3.57	22.6%
Europe	**£111.22**	**21.1%**	**£131.18**	**18.1%**

E-commerce turns 20 and my, how it's grown

By Chloe Rigby

Happy birthday e-commerce! We've now been able to shop online for 20 years. That's how long it is since Sting album *Ten Summoner's Tales* was bought in what's widely regarded as being the first secure online purchase. At the time, the album changed hands for $12.48 plus shipping on NetMarket. Today it's available for £4.46, plus shipping, on Amazon, and can be streamed for free on Spotify. So what else has changed since that first transaction on 11 August 1994?

The popularity of online shopping

This year the industry is likely to pass the £100 billion turnover milestone in the UK, having turned over £91 billion in 2013, according to IMRG figures.

ONS figures out last week found that 74% of all British adults have bought goods or services online.

As to why, Roger Brown, chief executive of personalisation specialist Peerius said: 'E-commerce and mobile technology have empowered consumers as they are no longer restricted to particular goods and services from one retailer or locality

as they can shop around different brands and even in different countries at their convenience.'

It's not online vs store, it's online + store

For years online appeared to be developing as an alternative to the high street. But more recently, consumers have started to take online into the store, using mobile devices there to check prices, availability and other factors. So-called showrooming got an initial frosty reception from retailers. Since then, however, it's become clear that helping customers to get the information they need in-store makes them more likely to buy. Retailers have responded by enabling shoppers to access information from their stores, whether that's by offering free Wi-Fi, enabling them to shop a wider range than the store can offer using in-store kiosks or iPads, or using the store as a collection point for online orders.

'Many high street retailers continue to thrive and understand how online shopping can complement in-store shopping and not compete,' said Peerius' Brown. 'Ultimately online is a digital store and is working towards the same business goals – to deliver an engaging shopping experience and drive sales. The mass adoption of mobile devices is forcing retailers to adapt rapidly to changing consumer behaviour and recent stats from IMRG also reveal that multichannel retailers are outperforming online-only retailers on mobile devices.'

The rise of m-commerce

While e-commerce has grown hugely in recent years, IMRG figures out as long ago as last September suggested mobile was already the main driver of growth. Smartphones and tablet computers, unimagined back in 1994, are growing in uptake, with a knock-on rise in popularity as devices for browsing and buying online.

As retailers have seen their traffic from mobile rise to more than 50%, they have responded by designing first for mobile, using responsive sites that can adapt depending on which viewing device is used. The industry is set to react quickly as 21st-century technology develops, and already many will be studying how retailers can best serve customers through emerging mobile devices such as Google Glass, only recently available in the UK.

Customer expectations

Remember when taking a pair of shoes back to the shop was likely to be met with a disdainful laugh? Today, serious footwear retailers offer free returns for their wares, understanding that shoppers just won't buy if they can't take it back. Digital retail has evolved in tandem with consumer behaviour as retailers move to respond to the way that technologically-enabled consumers want to buy. Largely, it seems, those customers want to buy wherever, whenever and however suits them – and for the lowest possible price.

'Today, having an online presence for retailers is just not enough,' said Martin Smethurst, managing director of retail at Wincor Nixdorf. 'Consumers now expect to be able to shop anywhere, anytime and anyhow they choose. This can mean any mixture of ordering in-store but being delivered to home, ordering online for home delivery, ordering online but collecting from the store, starting a transaction at home and picking that transaction up to complete when you reach the store. The possibilities are limitless.'

Peerius' Brown says that as online shopping develops, expectations will continue to grow. 'Online shopping enables consumers to browse freely, purchase quickly and find information easily wherever they are and on their preferred device,' he said. 'The rise of geo-location technology will further revolutionise both online and in-store shopping as consumers receive personalised messages in real-time to create an engaging experience however they prefer to purchase goods or services,' he said.

Convenient delivery

How the goods are delivered has become ever more important as the market has become more competitive. Back in 1994, being one of only a handful of online retailers (Amazon's roots go back to that year) could be enough to win the business of a determined digital shopper. Today some 16% of all non-food retail happens online and how quickly the goods can be delivered is critical in consumers' buying decisions.

Becky Clark, chief executive of parcel data management platform NetDespatch, said: 'Today, retailing is a multichannel experience underpinned by innovation and technology. The significant growth in the e-commerce market means that the delivery of goods has become an ever more important part of a retailer's customer service from both a speed, convenience and delivery perspective.

'The shift to conducting business online has led to a rise in volume and variety of packages, parcels and services handled by carriers. Right now, for a retailer to capitalise on the continued growth of online sales, it is essential that its chosen carrier is able to offer a range of services to suit the customer's increasingly diverse delivery requirements.'

12 August 2014

⇨ The above information is reprinted with kind permission from Internet Retailing. Please visit www.internetretailing.net for further information.

Four in ten consumers influenced by social media when researching products

Online retailers have seen evidence of their social media investments paying off with the revelation that 40% of consumers admit to being influenced by networks when buying online.

According to a new study from market researcher Mintel, 79% of consumers have viewed or shared content from a company's social media page. Younger browsers are most receptive to this particular form of advertising; the study finding that 21% of males aged 18–34 have bought a product straight after interacting with an ad on the likes of Facebook and Twitter.

What is perhaps more interesting for marketers is the rapid uptake in certain techniques within social media campaigns. Native advertising, for instance, is said to be growing immensely across networks as brands look for more subtle ways of making their presence felt.

Mintel went on to warn retailers to be patient with their activity on social media. Many consumers appear to be using networks for initial product research but it seems that very few are converting straight from a shared link.

Connecting brands with consumers

The findings indicated that social media is far more of an ice-breaker than a deal-clincher, as one quarter of networkers said they searched for a brand after seeing them advertised on social media. A total of 28% went one further by visiting a company's site in the moments after being exposed to their social ad.

A large proportion of these introductions may well be coming from Facebook, incidentally the world's most popular social network, which 86% of the study group visited at least once per week.

YouTube placed second in terms of popularity, on 60%, followed by Google+ (43%), Twitter (37%), LinkedIn (30%) and shopper-friendly networks Pinterest (30%) and Instagram (28%).

Unfortunately, a straight 50% of social network users claimed that company posts on such sites did not influence their product research. However, techniques like native advertising, or the very natural merger of sponsored content within related media, could provide brands with a way into their thought streams.

Spend continues to rise

Despite some shoppers appearing reluctant to gain product inspiration from social networks, Mintel technology analyst Bryant Harland said this would not stop brands from advertising on the channel.

'Social advertising spend is on the rise and shows no sign of slowing down,' he commented.

'Although third-party review websites and the brand's website are the top avenues for research overall, companies can still gain considerable traction by making product information readily available through social media.'

Overall spend on social media in the US is predicted to reach $11 billion by 2017 as brands look for ways of boosting their online fanbases.

August 2014

⇨ The above information is reprinted with kind permission from PerformanceIN. Please visit www.performancein.com for further information.

The science that makes us spend more in supermarkets, and feel good while we do it

An article from The Conversation.

By Graham Kendall, Professor of Operations Research and Vice-Provost at University of Nottingham

When you walk into a supermarket, you probably want to spend as little money as possible. The supermarket wants you to spend as much money as possible. Let battle commence.

As you enter the store your senses come under assault. You will often find that fresh produce (fruit, vegetables, flowers) is the first thing you see. The vibrant colours put you in a good mood, and the happier you are the more you are likely to spend.

Your sense of smell is also targeted. Freshly baked bread or roasting chickens reinforce how fresh the produce is and makes you feel hungry. You might even buy a chicken 'to save you the bother of cooking one yourself'. Even your sense of hearing may come under attack. Music with a slow rhythm tends to make you move slower, meaning you spend more time in the store.

Supermarkets exploit human nature to increase their profits. Have you ever wondered why items are sold in packs of 225g, rather than 250g? Cynics might argue that this is to make it more difficult to compare prices as we are working with unfamiliar weights. Supermarkets also rely on you not really checking what you are buying. You might assume that buying in bulk is more economic. This is not always the case. Besides, given that almost half of our food is believed to be thrown away, your savings might end up in the bin anyway.

Strategies such as those above get reported in the media on a regular basis. Mark Armstrong analysed retail discounting strategies for The Conversation last year, for example, and the *Daily Mail* recently published a feature on making 'rip offs look like bargains'.

You might think that awareness of these strategies would negate their effectiveness, but that doesn't appear to be the case. It would be a strong person that does not give way to an impulse buy occasionally and, for the supermarkets, the profits keep flowing.

Product placement

There are marketing strategies which you may not be aware of that also have an effect on our buying habits. Have you ever considered how supermarkets decide where to place items on the shelves and, more importantly, why they place them where they do?

When you see items on a supermarket shelf, you are actually looking at a planogram. A planogram is defined as a 'diagram or model that indicates the placement of retail products on shelves in order to maximise sales'.

Within these planograms, one phrase commonly used is 'eye level is buy level', indicating that products positioned at eye level are likely to sell better. You may find that the more expensive options are at eye level or just below, while the store's own brands are placed higher or lower on the shelves. Next time you are in a supermarket, just keep note of how many times you need to bend down, or stretch, to reach something you need. You might be surprised.

The 'number of facings', that is how many items of a product you can see, also has an effect on sales. The more visible a product, the higher the sales are likely to be. The location of goods in an aisle is also important. There is a school of thought that goods placed at the start of an aisle do not sell as well. A customer needs time to adjust to being in the aisle, so it takes a little time before they can decide what to buy.

Have you ever considered how supermarkets decide where to place items on the shelves and, more importantly, why they place them where they do?

You might think that designing a good planogram is about putting similar goods together; cereals, toiletries, baking goods and so on. However, supermarkets have found it makes sense to place some goods together even though they are not in the same category. Beer and crisps is an obvious example. If you are buying beer, crisps seem like a good idea, and convenience makes a purchase more likely. You may also find that they are the high-quality brands, but 'that's okay, why not treat ourselves?'

This idea of placing complementary goods together is a difficult problem. Beer and crisps might seem an easy choice but this could have an effect on the overall sales of crisps, especially if the space given to crisps in other parts of the store is reduced. And what do you do with peanuts, have them near the beer as well?

Supermarkets will also want customers to buy more expensive products – a process known as 'upselling'. If you want to persuade the customer to buy the more expensive brand of lager, how should you arrange the store? You still need to stock the cheaper options, for those that really are on a budget. But for the customers that can afford it, you want them to choose the premium product. Getting that balance right is not easy. My colleagues and I are among the researchers striving to develop the perfect algorithm taking into account size, height and depth of shelves, to direct customers to the right product, at the right time.

Shoppers won't always obey the science, but these techniques are retailers' most effective tools in the fight for our weekly budget. The battle between supermarkets and their customers continues.

4 March 2014

⇨ The above information is reprinted with kind permission from The Conversation. Please visit www.theconversation.com for further information.

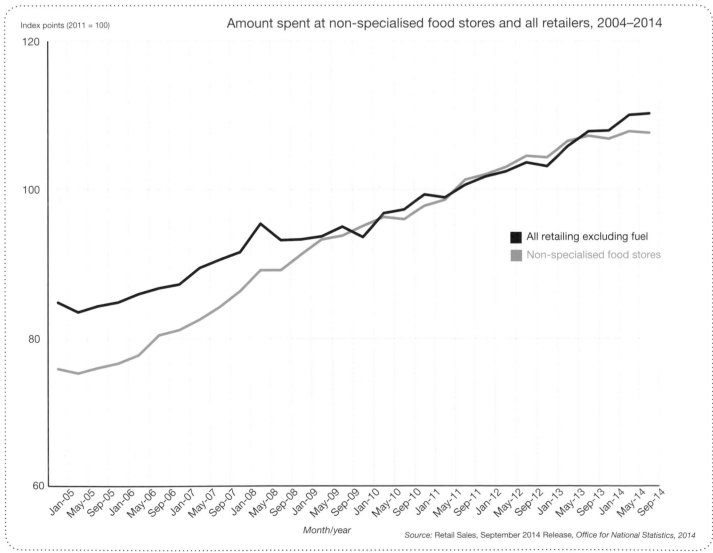

Amount spent at non-specialised food stores and all retailers, 2004–2014

Index points (2011 = 100)

Legend:
- All retailing excluding fuel
- Non-specialised food stores

Month/year

Source: Retail Sales, September 2014 Release, *Office for National Statistics, 2014*

Same-day delivery a new threat to retailers

By Scott Kirsner

I did something evil last Wednesday. Instead of walking two blocks to the Staples near my house to buy printer ink, or ten blocks to my neighbourhood bookstore to pick up a paperback that a friend recommended, I placed an order on Amazon.com and selected the 'same-day delivery' option. Just over nine hours later, an Amazon box appeared on my doorstep. The convenience cost me $11.97.

Why do I say evil? Because I appreciate having stores in my neighbourhood that keep the main drag vibrant and participate in the life of the community. And Amazon's same-day service is just the beginning of a new wave of experimentation that could pose yet another Darwinian challenge to brick-and-mortar businesses of all sizes.

eBay and Google are also testing the waters – though not yet in Boston – and last month Walmart hinted at an intriguing strategy that would involve inviting its customers to become volunteer couriers. In the same way that e-commerce and the digital delivery of books, videos, and music led to the demise of lots of companies (remember Mike's Movies, Strawberries and Borders?), this feels to retailers like a new threat.

'This is another way for the giants to make it difficult for the small guy to compete,' says Rick Henry, owner of Stellabella Toys, which operates four stores in the Boston area. 'They can afford to lose money on it while they figure out if it can work.'

Those with memories that stretch back a dozen or so years (or who have watched the documentary *e-Dreams*) will remember Kozmo.com. The start-up offered free delivery of videos, toiletries and snack foods in about an hour, thanks to a fleet of drivers and bike messengers. The company raised $250 million – including $60 million from Amazon – but couldn't make the economics of same-day delivery work. Kozmo was out of business by 2001.

This time around, there are once again start-ups trying to solve the puzzle of same-day delivery, such as Postmates, which raised $5 million last month. But most of the action centres on big companies with deep pockets. To get my recent order to me, Amazon relied on an existing distribution centre in Nashua, and a nationwide courier service called A-1 Express, which carried my box from there to Brookline.

eBay is building its own network of 'shopping valets' for its eBay Now mobile app, launched in August. They fetch merchandise from chain stores like Nordstrom and Best Buy, and deliver it for $5. Consumers can follow their progress on a map, and get an estimate of arrival time. Google is taking a similar approach in the San Francisco area with Google Shopping Express, which was unveiled last month. Framingham-based Staples is among its retail partners. The service's early users are getting six months of free, unlimited same-day delivery; regular pricing hasn't yet been announced.

Walmart began testing a same-day service called Walmart To Go last year in several metropolitan areas, for a $10 fee. And in a recent Reuters interview, Joel Anderson, chief executive of Walmart.com, suggested that the Arkansas-based chain might eventually turn some of its customers into a courier corps, offering discounts to shoppers willing to drop off an order or two on their way home.

'I'd think liability would be a big issue there,' says Jon Hurst, president of the Retailers Association of Massachusetts, a trade association with 3,500 members. 'How do you find the right customers you can trust to do that? It'll be interesting to see how and if they can work that out.'

Some businesses in Boston, including many stores that sell liquor or appliances, already offer same-day delivery. In Cambridge, the Harvard Book Store has had it as an option since 2009, priced at $5 for the first book, $1 for each additional book. Cargo bikes operated by Metro Pedal Power carry the merchandise.

Henry at Stellabella Toys says his business doesn't promote the same-day delivery, but he will do it in a pinch. 'I'm going to resist being pushed into it, because I don't think customers really want it,' he says. His focus: getting customers into his

stores to see the assortment of 6,000 items they carry.

The questions that remain unanswered are where the real price of same-day service will settle, and how many consumers will be willing to pay it. Venture capitalist Bob Davis, an investor in e-commerce companies, suggests that if Amazon figures out how to do it in a way that doesn't 'hit the customer in the pocketbook', they may be able to move into groceries, 'and that's when same-day achieves real relevance. You get groceries, nail polish and a new book.'

But Forrester Research analyst Sucharita Mulpuru believes that all of today's same-day services are operating at a loss, and that most consumers wouldn't be willing to pay the full price if it was passed on to them.

Let's fast-forward a few years. Amazon has already acquired a North Reading company, Kiva Systems, that sells warehouse robots that help fill online orders, and Amazon chief executive Jeff Bezos is an investor in a Boston company, Rethink Robotics, that makes a dextrous, two-armed robot named Baxter. Google is developing a self-driving car. Several companies, including a new Harvard Business School start-up called Daedalus Systems, are considering using airborne, battery-powered drones to deliver small packages – once the Federal Aviation Administration establishes guidelines.

In other words, the FedEx of the instant gratification age may not need pilots, distribution centre workers or drivers on its payroll.

7 April 2013

⇨ The above information is reprinted with kind permission from *The Boston Globe*. Please visit www.bostonglobe.com for further information.

The tricky business of advertising to children

As Subway launches a multi-million-dollar healthy eating ad campaign aimed at kids, is marketing to children harmful or a useful tool for teaching critical analysis?

By Bruce Watson

In the US, the average child watches an estimated 16,000 television commercials a year. And, while US children are among the world's most avid consumers of advertising, the effect of television on children is a concern for parents across the globe.

Critics of advertising claim that it contributes to a host of ills, from childhood obesity and poor impulse control to precocious sexuality. Proponents say advertising can be a useful tool for teaching children about critical analysis.

Recently, the battle for the hearts and minds of America's children opened a new front: their stomachs. Allying itself with Michelle Obama's campaign against childhood obesity, fast-food company Subway has agreed to spend $41 million over three years to promote a healthy-eating programme aimed at children.

The advertising campaign, with the slogan 'Playtime: Powered by Veggies', represents Subway's most aggressive child marketing attempt to date. By comparison, the company spent $2.2 million on child marketing in 2011 and $7 million in 2012. The same year, McDonald's spent an estimated $42 million on ad buys for its Happy Meals.

Subway's campaign offers a fresh angle on an old issue, namely the question of whether or not it is ethical for corporations to directly market to children. In some ways, the restaurant is a perfect test case; while the nutritional profile of Subway's offerings is far from perfect, it is one of the healthier options in the large-chain fast-food market. And, by presenting an aggressively marketed alternative to McDonald's, Subway is suggesting an enemy-of-my-enemy-is-my-friend strategy that could create some strange bedfellows in the war against childhood obesity.

On the other hand, regardless of the healthiness of Subway's offerings, they are still being directly marketed to children, a strategy many parents consider problematic. Susan Linn, director of the Campaign for a Commercial-Free Childhood, questions the very nature of child marketing.

Advertisement

'There's no moral, ethical, or social justification for marketing any product to children,' she says. 'Advertising healthier foods to children is problematic. We want children to develop a healthy relationship to nutrition and to the foods that they consume. Advertising trains kids to choose foods based on celebrity, not based on what's on the package.'

Ian Barber, communications director of the UK's Advertising Association, suggests that the child marketing furore may ultimately be a matter of displacement; parents who are concerned about certain products may become angry or upset when they are marketed to children, and may blame the medium for the message.

'Advertising becomes a proxy for complaints about particular companies, brands or products,' he argues. 'Advertising isn't the issue. The sort of advertisements that children see is the issue. But then you get into a very objective debate about how people feel about certain brands or services.'

Linn disagrees. 'Advertising, in and of itself, is harmful to children,' she argues. 'Marketing targets emotions, not intellect. It trains children to choose products not for the actual value of the product, but because of celebrity or what's on the package. It undermines critical thinking and promotes impulse buying.'

When it comes to legal restrictions on child advertising, the UK occupies a spot somewhere near the middle of the spectrum. At one extreme, Sweden, Norway and Quebec completely bar marketing to children under the age of 12. At the opposite end are countries such as the US, where the marketing industry is self-regulated, with few legal restrictions on the material that advertisers can broadcast to children.

In Britain, the advertising industry self-regulates, within the bounds of certain national and international laws that limit the products and techniques that it is allowed to employ. 'For example, you cannot make a child feel inferior or unpopular for not buying a product,' Barbour explains. 'You can't take advantage of their credulity, or suggest that they're lacking in courage or loyalty. You can't encourage them to actively pester their parents, or make a direct exhortation to a child to buy a product.' Some of these rules, he emphasises, are based in laws, but many are self-imposed by the advertising industry.

For consumers in countries where advertising is less strictly regulated, the UK's advertising standards may seem almost genteel. Then again, Barber claims, the British advertising industry has experienced few complaints from parents. 'The proportion of complaints about ads that relate to concerns about children is minuscule,' he says. 'In fact, the all-time number-one complained about ad in the UK was for Kentucky Fried Chicken, and the reason was that people in the commercial were speaking with their mouths full.'

Another approach for ameliorating the effect of child advertising may lie in teaching children how to understand the media messages that constantly barrage them. Media Smart, an organisation funded by Barber's advertising lobby, approaches the issue of child marketing from the perspective of education. 'Media Smart helps kids better understand what advertising is, how advertising works, what its intentions are, and how to be critical of it,' Barbour explains. 'Seeking to shield children completely from advertising doesn't seem like a pragmatic or helpful response to any concerns that you might have. Our approach is to make sure the advertising targeted to kids is appropriate, and help kids to understand what advertising does.'

From this perspective, advertising can be a useful tool for teaching children to be cynical and careful consumers of cultural messages. Then again, as the advertising lobby's own research (PDF) has shown, children are not capable of understanding the 'commercial intent' of advertising until they reach the age of 12.

Linn questions the value of media literacy training. 'I agree that it's important to teach children critical thinking skills,' she says. 'But to depend on children to protect themselves from advertising is either naïve or disingenuous.' More to the point, she argues, it's unclear that media literacy can influence consumer behaviour. 'There's research showing that media literacy can inculcate scepticism, but there's no link between scepticism and consumer behaviour.'

Ultimately, Linn notes, 'there's no evidence that advertising is beneficial'. More to the point, she argues, it erodes children's creative play. 'That's the foundation of learning creativity and constructive problem solving, both of which are essential to a democratic society.' In other words, Linn suggests, for all its benefits, Subway's better nutrition campaign may be yet another tool for eating away at the core values of society.

24 February 2014

⇨ The above information is reprinted with kind permission from *The Guardian*. Please visit www.theguardian.com for further information.

Food giants target children with addictive 'advergames'

By Chris Green

Addictive online games used by food and drinks firms to target children are undermining efforts to counter obesity and should be subject to much tougher rules, local health chiefs say today.

The Local Government Association (LGA), which represents almost 400 councils in England and Wales, is calling for pop-up health warnings to accompany the 'advergames', which it says plug products containing high levels of sugars, salts and fats to young children.

Swizzels Matlow, Chewits and Weetos are a few of the well-known brands to have placed the free games on their websites. According to the LGA, they are increasingly easy to access by children using smartphones and tablet computers.

The Advertising Standards Authority (ASA) is currently able to take action against a company if a game 'encourages poor nutritional habits, such as excessive consumption or unhealthy lifestyles'. But the LGA says the rules do not go far enough and wants health warnings to flash up before each one begins.

Cllr Katie Hall, Chair of the LGA's Community Wellbeing Board, said: 'It is unacceptable for food giants to be targeting children with these addictive games. Food manufacturers are weaning youngsters onto a diet laden with sugar, fat and salt – creating the next generation of unhealthy children.'

A report commissioned by the Family and Parenting Institute, published in 2012, suggested that children's brains process advergames in a different way from traditional adverts, on a 'subconscious, emotional' level.

'The result of this is that advergames can change children's behaviour without their conscious awareness,' the authors wrote. 'This raises fundamental ethical questions about the technique, particularly in view of the fact that they appear to be widely used for food and drink products high in salt, sugar and fat. There is a serious health concern if children's food choices are influenced subconsciously.'

Dr Haiming Hang, Senior Lecturer in Marketing at the University of Bath and one of the report's authors, told *The Independent* that children did not understand the games were adverts and had no 'cognitive defence' to the food firms' marketing.

Swizzles Matlow, which makes sweets including Love Hearts, Refreshers and Drumstick lollies, has several games on its website including 'Bubble Burster', where players fly a remote-control probe through a vat of Refreshers mix, popping bubbles.

The Chewits sweets website has a fortune telling game called 'Mystic Chewie', which uses the slogan 'I predict you'll be hooked', as well as a skill game called The Claw.

Stuart Lane, commercial director for the UK and Ireland at Cloetta, which makes Chewits, said the company was 'very sensitive to the debate' around advergames but strived to be a 'responsible manufacturer'. He added: 'If the ASA decided to change the rules around this, we'd follow them.'

The Weetos cereal website features a game called 'Kitchen Assault' in which players guide one of the chocolate-flavoured hoops around an obstacle course.

Weetabix, which makes Weetos, said in a statement: 'Weetabix is committed to meeting or exceeding all the guidelines and statutory requirements on advertising to children and strongly believes in responsible marketing.'

The flavoured milk brand Nesquik also has sports games on its website featuring its rabbit mascot. A spokeswoman for manufacturers Nestlé said the games featured on its US website and not the UK version, adding: 'As the world's leading nutrition, health and wellness company, we have a strict policy on marketing and advertising to children.'

But Dr Hang said British children could easily be playing the games on foreign websites: 'When kids play advergames on a website, they don't say: "OK, this is an American website, I'm not going to play it." They just play games.'

Luciana Berger MP, Labour's shadow Public Health Minister, said she was 'alarmed' by the increasing use of advergames. 'Parents are anxious about these unfamiliar techniques in new online media and more must be done to ensure they have the information they need to protect their children from being bombarded by these compelling free games that we know most children don't even recognise as adverts,' she added.

In a statement, the ASA said: 'Advergames by food companies have to stick to strict rules. We've banned advergames that promoted overeating and will not hesitate to ban any others that encourage unhealthy diets or lifestyles. We've also issued clear guidance to advertisers to help them prepare their advergames responsibly.'

Jeremy Dee, managing director of Swizzels Matlow, said: 'The games on our website are light-hearted and engaging and are simply our way of providing something fun for the family to enjoy together. We never target children directly with advertising.'

29 March 2014

⇨ The above information is reprinted with kind permission from *The Independent*. Please visit www.independent.co.uk for further information.

Branded for life? Researchers examine impact of consumer culture on UK's children

Consumers of fashionable brands, the latest gadgets and the coolest looks are getting ever younger. Yet, children who immerse themselves in consumer culture feel worse about themselves, not better, say researchers at the University of Sussex.

The Children's Consumer Culture Project at the University has involved three years of work with 1,500 children to investigate how materialistic and appearance-focused values develop in childhood, and to study the impact of consumer culture and advertising messages about what is 'cool' and beautiful on children's well-being.

The project's preliminary research findings will be shared today (3 May 2013) with researchers, policy makers and diverse organisations at a special event[1] at the University. The opening address will be given by Caroline Lucas MP, and attendees include teachers, schools representatives, social, educational and clinical psychologists, academics, and charity representatives.

The project, funded by the Leverhulme Trust and led by University of Sussex psychologists Dr Helga Dittmar and Professor Robin Banerjee, combines in-depth interviews with children and large-scale surveys and experiments to assess the impact of exposure to consumer culture on children aged eight to 14 years.

The project assesses how children respond to consumer culture and advertising, which dictate what is beautiful, desirable and cool, and examines whether such aspirations lead to lower self-esteem and lower well-being in children.

Results show that children with lower well-being are more drawn to the consumer culture value system, seeing improvements to physical appearance and material possessions as a route to making gains in their social status. Yet these efforts in fact are likely to be counter-productive. The research team has shown that, over time, those who strive to achieve consumer culture ideals become more rejected within their peer groups and end up feeling worse overall.

The conference and research findings are timely. The *Bailey Review of the Commercialisation and Sexualisation of Childhood* was published on 6 June 2011 and a government assessment of progress made so far in implementing its recommendations is due to be published. Furthermore, in April 2013 a campaign was launched 'Leave Our Kids Alone', petitioning for advertising aimed at under-12s to be banned.

Here, Helga Dittmar and Robin Banerjee discuss the reasons behind the research and their findings.

Why is it important to study consumer culture, children and well-being?

Robin: Many children see consumer culture as a way of gaining acceptance and social status among their peers, believing that 'you are liked more if you have cool things and look good'. In fact, we have found that children who already feel bad about themselves are more likely to turn to consumer culture values for answers, even though these values are detrimental to their body esteem, their emotional functioning and their subjective well-being. In contrast, children who feel secure in their identity are buffered against such a downward spiral.

What is new in what you are saying?

Helga: The relationship of consumer culture values with lower well-being is well-documented in adults, but there is hardly any research on children, even though concern about the detrimental effects on children's well-being is rising. We are investigating body image concerns and materialistic values as twin, interlinked, core components of contemporary consumer culture that are particularly relevant to young people today.

Having studied more than 1,000 children for over two years, we are also able to address – for the very first time – the pressing question of how the links play out over time between the idealised body images and acquisitive impulses of consumer culture on the one hand, and the identity and well-being of children on the other.

How could law/government/society/individuals tackle any negative associations for children with regard to consumer culture?

Helga: The materialistic and appearance-focused values that British consumer culture promotes can be detrimental to children's well-being, which may help to explain why British children emerged with low scores of well-being in a UNICEF report published this month (16th out of the 27 richest countries, below Slovenia and Portugal).

International differences in advertising regulations may also play a role: for example, in Norway and Sweden, television advertising aimed at children aged below 12 is banned. Advertising and media regulations, such as those recommended in the Bailey Review and by the Leave Our Kids Alone campaign, may help to address the negative impact of consumer culture on children's well-being here in Britain.

The Government's Body Confidence Campaign aims to promote positive body image among society, parents, and young people, an intention echoed in various media innovations (such as Channel 4's 4Beauty web site).

The University of Sussex research findings also underline the importance of raising awareness about the effects of consumer culture in contemporary Britain. Children can be helped – both at home and at school – and may even be able to help themselves and their peers, to put consumer culture into perspective, and to learn about the qualities that really underpin positive social relationships, emotional health and general well-being.

Notes for editors

1 Consumer culture and children's well-being event, University of Sussex, Friday 3 May 9:00 until 16:00, University of Sussex Conference Centre.

To ask a question or book a place email: consumercultureproject@ sussex.ac.uk.

Visit the project website: www.sussex.ac.uk/psychology consumercultureproject.

University of Sussex Press office contacts: Maggie Clune and Jacqui Bealing. Tel: 01273 678 888. Email: press@sussex.ac.uk.

View press releases online at: http:// www.sussex.ac.uk/newsandevents/.

29 October 2014

⇨ The above information is reprinted with kind permission from the University of Sussex. Please visit www.sussex.ac.uk for further information.

BrandIndex Rankings 2013

YouGov's BrandIndex Rankings compare BrandIndex Buzz scores for over 850 brands in 34 categories, to reveal the UK brands with the most positive brand noise during the last 12 months.

All of the brands were rated using YouGov BrandIndex's Buzz score. YouGov BrandIndex runs 3,700 daily interviews and asks respondents their views about brands. Buzz scores are worked out by asking if respondents have heard anything positive or negative about a brand in the last two weeks, through advertising, news, word-of-mouth or friends and family. Buzz scores measure recent brand sentiment and also indicate the direction of recent awareness.

Once again, according to YouGov BrandIndex, BBC iPlayer is the overall number one in terms of consumer perception, maintaining its position from 2012. Samsung has risen the most places as it appears in second, up from ninth the previous year. Rival, Apple iPad, drops out of the top ten completely. The highest new entry on the chart was Aldi, making it the highest ranking supermarket, reflecting the change in perception it has achieved.

Netflix has seen the largest increase in its YouGov BrandIndex Buzz score in 2013, up from fifth last year. MoneyGram is the highest new entry. London Underground was at number one half way through the year, before finally settling in 4th position. Perhaps news of strikes, price increases and job losses can explain this fall. This year's list is notable for the absence of energy companies, of which there were five in last year's list. We can attribute this to price increases above inflation across the 'big six'.

#1 BBC iPlayer For the second consecutive year at the top of the rankings, BBC iPlayer clearly shows its persistent appeal for UK customers.

#2 John Lewis Continuing its upward trend in our ranking, John Lewis once again proved its popularity among British shoppers.

#2 Samsung Samsung's huge launch campaigns around the Galaxy S4 Smartphone, and the NX Android Camera in 2013 helped the brand rising to a joint 2nd position in our latest rankings.

#4 Aldi Aldi is a new entry at number 4 this year, making it the highest ranking supermarket in our list.

#5 Dyson Home appliance company Dyson was the first new entry on our 2013 mid-year rankings and the brand has kept its position for the remainder of 2013.

#6 Marks & Spencer Marks & Spencer remains in our top ten due in no small part to its successful food division, which is continuing to perform well.

#7 BBC.co.uk The online section of the BBC makes a new appearance in the rankings to complement the top spot that the BBC iPlayer service holds.

#8 Waitrose Moving up a place from last year's rankings, Waitrose continues to appeal to customers who seek out quality.

#9 Sainsbury's A retention of the same position in the rankings for Sainsbury's this year, the company looked to introduce several initiatives to complement its well-established 'Live Well For Less' and 'Brand Match' message.

#10 YouTube Another new entry into the top ten this year, YouTube continues to grow and find ways to interact with users.

2013

⇨ The above information is reprinted with kind permission from YouGov. Please viist www. brandindex.com for further information.

Consumer contracts regulations

From 13 June 2014 the Consumer Contracts Regulations, which implement the Consumer Rights Directive in UK law, came into effect.

The regulations apply to items bought online, at a distance, or away from a trader's premises (for example, at home or at work).

They replace the Distance Selling Regulations and Doorstep Selling Regulations. They also make it an obligation for traders to give consumers certain information.

Information you should expect

The Consumer Contracts (Information, Cancellation and Additional Charges) Regulations 2013, as they are referred to in full, require traders to give you certain information.

The specific information varies depending on whether the sale is made at a distance or face-to-face or in store.

At a distance or face-to-face off-premises

The following key information has to be given:

⇨ a description of the goods or service, including how long any commitment will last on the part of the consumer

⇨ the total price of the goods or service, or the manner in which the price will be calculated if this can't be determined

⇨ cost of delivery and details of who pays for the cost of returning items if you have a right to cancel and change your mind

⇨ details of any right to cancel – the trader also needs to provide, or make available, a standard cancellation form to make cancelling easy (although you aren't under any obligation to use it)

⇨ information about the seller, including their geographical address and phone number

⇨ information on the compatibility of digital content with hardware and other software is also part of the information traders are obliged to provide.

Delivery of key information

Failure to provide the required information, or to provide it in the way set out in the regulations, could result in cancellation rights being extended by up to a year.

The information should be given on paper unless you agree to take it on some other 'durable medium' like email, for example.

It can be provided in a way appropriate to the means of communication, so verbally if the contract is made by phone.

You are also entitled to confirmation of the contract and if the information wasn't initially provided in a durable form, the trader must provide it at the point of confirmation.

On-premises sales

The trader doesn't have to provide as much information in this instance, but it must still provide certain information.

For example, information about the goods or services being bought, the price, the compatibility of digital

content and details of any delivery costs.

Summary

⇨ Your right to cancel an order starts the moment you place your order and ends 14 days from the day you receive it.

⇨ Your right to cancel a service starts the moment you enter into the contract and lasts 14 days.

⇨ If you want to download digital content within the 14-day cancellation period you must agree to waive your cancellation rights.

⇨ Companies are not allowed to charge you for items they put in your online shopping basket or that you have bought as a result of a pre-ticked box.

Cancelling goods

Your right to cancel

Your right to cancel an order for goods starts the moment you place your order and ends 14 days from the day you receive your goods.

If your order consists of multiple goods, the 14 days runs from when you get the last of the batch.

This 14-day period is the time you have to decide whether to cancel, you then have a further 14 days to actually send the goods back.

Your right to a refund

You should get a refund within 14 days of either the trader getting the goods back, or you providing evidence of having returned the goods (for example, a proof of postage receipt from the post office), whichever is the sooner.

A deduction can be made if the value of the goods has been reduced as a result of you handling the goods more than was necessary.

The extent to which a customer can handle the goods is the same as it would be if you were assessing them in a shop.

Refunding the cost of delivery

The trader has to refund the basic delivery cost of getting the goods to you in the first place, so if you opted for enhanced service, e.g. guaranteed next day, it only has to refund the basic cost.

Exemptions

There are some circumstances where the Consumer Contracts Regulations won't give you a right to cancel.

These include, CDs, DVDs or software if you've broken the seal on the wrapping, perishable items, tailor-made or personalised items.

Also included are goods that have been mixed inseparably with other items after delivery.

Always check the t&cs

14 days is the minimum cancellation period that consumers must be given and many sellers choose to exceed this, so always check the terms and conditions in case you have longer to change your mind.

Cancelling services

Your right to cancel

You have 14 days from entering into a service contract in which you can cancel it.

The trader shouldn't start providing the service before the 14-day cancellation period has ended, unless you have requested this.

If you request a service starts straightaway

In this instance you will still have the right to cancel, but you must pay for the value of the service that is provided up to the point you cancel.

For example, if you buy a service like gym membership and start using the gym and then change your mind within this 14-day time period, you will be refunded but could be charged for the amount of gym time you used.

If the service is provided in full within 14 days

The right to cancel can be lost during the cancellation period if the service is provided in full before the 14 days elapses.

Exemptions

There are some contracts where you won't have a right to cancel a service. For example, hotel bookings, flights, car hire, concerts and other event tickets, or where the trader is carrying out urgent repairs or maintenance.

Always check the t&cs

14 days is the minimum cancellation period that consumers must be given and many sellers choose to exceed this, so always check the terms and conditions in case you have longer to change your mind.

Cancelling digital downloads

The Consumer Contracts Regulations contain specific provisions for digital content.

Retailers must not supply digital content, such as music or software downloads, within the 14-day cancellation period, unless the consumer has given their express consent to this happening.

The consumer must also acknowledge that once the download starts they will lose their right to cancel.

If a consumer doesn't give their consent, they have to wait until the cancellation period has ended before they can download the digital content.

This is to ensure the digital content is what you want before downloading it.

Pre-ticked boxes

The Consumer Contracts Regulations make it clear that a trader won't be able to charge a consumer for an item where it was selected for the consumer as part of that purchasing process, rather than the consumer actively choosing to add it to their basket.

For example, retailers are not allowed to charge for an extended warranty if it was added into your basket as a result of a pre-ticked box.

If a company does charge you in this way, you are entitled to your money back.

Delivery of goods

The Consumer Contracts Regulations say that goods must be delivered within the time frame you agree with the seller.

If no time frame is agreed, the seller has to deliver 'without undue delay' and at the very latest not more than 30 days from the day after the contract is made.

The Consumer Contracts Regulations make it clear that the seller is responsible for the condition of the goods until the goods are received by the consumer, or by someone else they have nominated to receive them on their behalf, like a neighbour.

Check the t&cs to ensure that you are not agreeing to a neighbour receiving your order without your explicit consent.

Returning faulty goods

If you receive faulty goods and wish to return them, The Consumer Contracts Regulations are in addition to your other legal rights.

So, if your goods are faulty and don't do what they're supposed to, or don't match the description given, you have the same consumer rights under the Sale of Goods Act as you have when buying in store.

Any terms and conditions that say you must cover the cost of returning an item wouldn't apply where the goods being returned are faulty.

Excessive call charges

The Consumer Contracts Regulations also prohibits helpline phone charges in excess of the basic rate for calls by existing customers to the retailer or trader about products purchased.

For example, if you are ringing to make a complaint, enquire about your order, or to cancel your order, retailers can't use premium rate numbers. They must provide a basic rate number for you to call.

The same applies to energy supplier customers. You must be provided with a basic rate number to call if you have an enquiry or complaint about your account.

If you do have to call a company on a surcharged number about goods or services you have bought, or have agreed to buy, you have the automatic legal right to claim back the surcharge from the company.

These rules do not apply to sales calls.

⇨ The above information is reprinted with kind permission from *Which?* Please visit www.which.co.uk for further information.

Three key facts about the Consumer Contracts Regulations

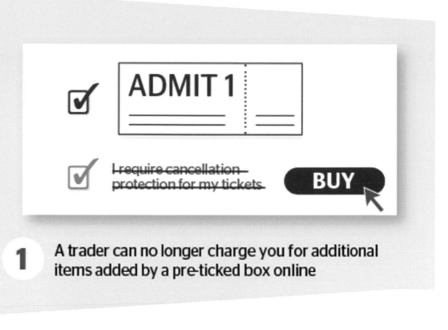

1 A trader can no longer charge you for additional items added by a pre-ticked box online

2 You can cancel a service contract online, such as a gym membership, 14 days after you enter it

3 You should get a refund within 14 days of cancelling goods or services online or within 14 days of returning the goods to the trader

Which?

Accepting returns and giving refunds: the law

You must offer a full refund if an item is faulty, not as described or doesn't do what it's supposed to.

When you don't have to offer a refund

You don't have to refund a customer if they:

⇨ knew an item was faulty when they bought it

⇨ damaged an item by trying to repair it themselves or getting someone else to do it (though they may still have the right to a repair, replacement or partial refund)

⇨ no longer want an item (e.g. because it's the wrong size or colour) unless they bought it without seeing it.

You have to offer a refund for certain items only if they're faulty, e.g.:

⇨ personalised items and custom-made items, e.g. curtains

⇨ perishable items, e.g. frozen food or flowers

⇨ newspapers and magazines

⇨ unwrapped CDs, DVDs and computer software.

Customers have exactly the same rights to refunds when they buy items in a sale as when they buy them at full price.

Online, mail and phone order sales

Online, mail and telephone order customers have the right to cancel for a limited time even if the goods aren't faulty. Sales of this kind are known as 'distance selling'.

You must offer a refund to customers if they return goods within 14 days of receiving them.

You must then refund the customer within 14 days of receiving the goods back. They don't have to provide a reason.

Repairs and replacements

If a customer has 'accepted' an item, but later discovers a fault, you may have to repair or replace it. The customer can still reject the item after it's been repaired or replaced.

A customer has accepted an item if they've:

⇨ told you they've accepted it (having had enough opportunity to inspect the item before confirming they've received it)

⇨ altered the item.

You must repair or replace an item if a customer returns it within six months – unless you can prove it wasn't faulty when they bought it.

You can ask a customer to prove an item was faulty when they bought it if they ask for a repair or replacement after six months.

Customers have up to six years to make a claim for an item they've bought from you (five years in Scotland).

Warranties and guarantees

A customer has the same right to free repairs or a replacement regardless of whether they have a warranty or guarantee or not. So you may still have to repair or replace goods if a customer's warranty or guarantee has run out.

Proof of purchase

You can ask the customer for proof that they bought an item from you. This could be a sales receipt or other evidence such as a bank statement or packaging.

Items returned by someone other than the buyer

You only have to accept returns from the person who bought the item.

Penalties for displaying notices

It's illegal to display any notice that deliberately misleads consumers or deceives them about their rights, e.g. a sign that says you don't accept returns or offer refunds.

⇨ The above information is reprinted with kind permission from GOV.UK.

© Crown copyright 2014

Sir, are you sure you didn't drop it in the toilet?

No really, it must've been like that when I bought it.

Excuse no. 203

Online and distance selling for businesses

1. Overview

You must provide certain information for your customers if you're selling goods online, through digital TV, by mail order or by phone, text message or fax.

Before an order is placed

All distance sellers must follow certain rules before and after an order is placed.

You must display information such as:

⇨ your business name and contact details

⇨ a description of your goods or services

⇨ the price, including all taxes

⇨ how a customer can pay

⇨ delivery arrangements, costs and how long goods will take to arrive

⇨ the minimum length of their contract

⇨ conditions for terminating contracts

⇨ information about the customer's right to cancel within 14 days.

You must tell the customer if they will be responsible for paying for the return of goods if they cancel. If you don't, they're not liable for the costs.

After an order is placed

You must get in touch with your customer in writing after an order is placed and before the goods or services have been delivered.

You must tell them:

⇨ details of what they have purchased

⇨ the total cost

⇨ arrangements for delivery

⇨ the minimum duration of any contract and arrangements for terminating the contract

⇨ how and when they can cancel an order and who pays for returning goods

⇨ an address where complaints can be sent

⇨ any guarantees or after-sales services you offer

⇨ conditions for terminating contracts

⇨ any helpline call charges that are more than calling an 01, 02 or 03 number, or a mobile or free number.

There are extra rules if you're selling online or selling overseas.

Sale of Goods Act

All businesses that supply goods, including online and distance sellers, must follow the 'Sale of Goods Act'.

You could be classed as a trader if you sell goods or services. If you're trading, you're self-employed.

2. Selling online

As well as the general rules for distance selling, there are some extra rules for selling online.

You must:

⇨ list the steps involved in a customer placing an order

⇨ acknowledge receipt of any orders electronically as soon as possible

⇨ take reasonable steps to allow customers to correct any errors in their order

⇨ let customers know what languages are available to them

⇨ make sure customers can store and reproduce your terms and conditions, i.e. these can be downloaded and printed off

⇨ give your email address

⇨ give your VAT number (if your business is registered for VAT)

⇨ give clear prices and delivery costs for your products.

3. Selling overseas

As well as the general rules for distance selling, there are some extra rules for selling overseas.

Selling within the EU

You must charge VAT to EU customers if you'd do the same for customers in the UK.

Selling outside of the EU

You must not charge VAT for customers outside of the EU. Instead, fill out a customs declaration when you ship the products.

You must keep 'proof of export' if you sell to customers outside of the EU. This includes:

⇨ the customer's order – including their name, VAT number and delivery address

⇨ internal correspondence

⇨ sales invoices

⇨ advice notes

⇨ packing lists

⇨ commercial transport documents

⇨ details of insurance or freight charges

⇨ bank statements

⇨ consignment notes.

⇨ The above information is reprinted with kind permission from GOV.UK.

Key facts on the new EU Consumer Rights Directive

In the EU, consumer protection legislation guarantees that everyone has the right to be treated fairly when buying goods at the supermarket, paying the bill with the energy supplier or downloading music.

The Charter of Fundamental Rights, the European treaties and sector-specific EU legislation all guarantee a high level of consumer protection in the EU. European legislation guarantees consumers fair treatment, products which meet acceptable standards and a right of redress if something goes wrong.

These rules cover domestic and cross-border trade, combat unfair practices and give consumers the right to cancel the purchases they made online or which they have made on the high street. But despite these successes, EU consumers do not always feel adequately protected and confident about making purchases, especially online and/or across borders. As consumer expenditure accounts for 56% of EU GDP, boosting consumer confidence can directly translate into boosting economic growth.

The new EU Consumer Rights Directive – which applies in all Member States from 13 June 2014 – will strengthen consumer rights by giving customers the same rights across the EU, while striking the right balance between consumer protection and business competitiveness.

What are the main advantages of the new consumer rules?

⇨ They align and harmonise national consumer rules in several important areas, such as on the information consumers need to get before they purchase something, and their right to cancel online purchases. Increased harmonisation means that consumers can rely on the same rights, whether they shop in the EU or in the UK.

⇨ They strengthen consumer rights, ensuring a higher level of protection regardless of whether consumers are shopping on the high street or online, in their own country or elsewhere in the EU. For example, consumers will now have clearer information on prices, wherever and whichever way they shop, as traders will have to disclose the total cost of the product or service, as well as any extra fees.

How do the new rules help shoppers?

⇨ No more cost-traps on the Internet. From now on, online shoppers need to confirm that they accept paying for something before they are charged. It must be clearly indicated what is included in the price you are paying.

⇨ No more pre-ticked boxes. Currently consumers shopping online may end up paying for services they don't want (such as priority boarding on planes), because they forget to un-tick boxes on websites. The new Consumer Rights Directive introduces a clear ban on pre-ticked boxes on websites for charging additional payments.

⇨ Online shoppers will not have to pay for charges of which they are not clearly informed before they make the purchase.

⇨ Traders will not be allowed to charge more for credit card payments than it costs them to provide such a payment option.

⇨ Traders operating hotlines for consumer complaints or questions, will not be able to charge more than the basic rate for such calls.

What about changing your mind and getting refunded?

The period for consumers to pull out of any distance purchase (e.g. something bought online) or off-premises (such as when a seller visits the consumer's home) is extended from the previous minimum seven days, to a uniform 14 days across the EU. These 14 days start counting from the day the consumer receives the goods, and the consumer has the right to cancel the purchase for any reason. When a seller hasn't clearly informed the consumer about the right to cancel the purchases, the return period will be extended a year.

Consumers will now also be allowed to pull out from purchases after solicited visits from sellers and from online auction purchases from professional sellers.

Traders must refund consumers within 14 days of cancellation, including standard delivery costs. Regarding goods, the trader can postpone the reimbursement until the goods are returned by the

consumer or the consumer provides evidence that these goods have been sent to the trader.

Consumers will be given a standard EU form to use if they want to cancel their purchases. This will make it easier for them to get out of contracts concluded outside of their home country.

Traders wanting consumers to pay for the return of goods after cancellation must clearly inform them beforehand, and give at least an estimate of the cost of returning bulky goods.

Does the Consumer Rights Directive do anything about purchases of digital products?

Anyone buying digital content will be able to get clearer information, including about details on which software and hardware the content works with, as well as information on copyright protections.

Consumers will be able to pull out of purchases of digital content up to the point where downloading or streaming of the content begins.

Are there any implications for businesses?

Common rules for businesses will make it easier for them to trade all over Europe.

Businesses making sales by phone, mail or online, or away from their premises, will now have a single set of rules to follow. This creates a level-playing field and cuts cross-border transaction costs.

As regards small businesses and craftsmen, there will be no right to pull out of a contract for urgent repairs and maintenance jobs. Member States can also exempt traders doing repairs or maintenance jobs in customers' homes for less than €200 from certain information requirements.

June 2014

⇨ The above information is reprinted with kind permission from the European Commission. Please visit ec.europa.eu for further information.

What are my rights when buying digital content?

The Consumer Rights Bill sets out what rights and remedies you would have when you pay for digital content. It clarifies that digital content would have to be:

⇨ of satisfactory quality,

⇨ fit for purpose, and

⇨ meet any description.

If the digital content didn't meet these quality rights, you would be entitled to a repair or a replacement of the digital content where practical, or failing that (that is, if the repair or replacement would take an unreasonable amount of time or cannot be done without significantly inconveniencing you), you would be entitled to some money back. You would only be entitled to return the faulty digital content for an immediate refund if the digital content was in a physical item (e.g. it is on a disc or embedded in goods such as a digital camera).

Other digital content rights would allow the trader to update the digital content within the terms of the contract, entitle you to a refund if the trader sold you the digital content without having the right to do so, and entitle you to a repair (if possible) or limited compensation if the trader fails to use reasonable care and skill to prevent the digital content (whether free or paid for) from damaging your device or other digital content.

My ebook's not working as I was told it would. What can I do?

You have downloaded an interactive ebook for your children and they have really enjoyed playing it and interacting with the characters in the book. Now you download a second ebook also described as having 'fully interactive content' but this time, although the characters are animated, all you can do is move through the pages in the book. The content is simply

not interactive. The book therefore does not meet its description. Under the Bill you would be entitled to a repair or replacement of the ebook to bring it into line with how it was described. If this does not resolve the issue, you would be entitled to keep the ebook but to have some money back.

My cloud-based software's not working properly. What can I do?

You pay to access some software on the cloud, but it is not streaming properly to your device. You are sure the problem isn't with your bandwidth, your ISP or with your device, because you are still able to stream movies successfully. It is only accessing this software that is a problem – it is not of satisfactory quality. You would be entitled to a repair or replacement of the digital content. As this is a time-specific issue repair/replacement may not be possible so you would be entitled to some money back.

My MP3 keeps stopping, what can I do?

You pay to download a music file but it keeps stopping halfway through. You are sure that this is not a problem with your ISP service or with your device. You would be entitled to a repair or a replacement of the file. In practice this would probably mean you would get another download. You would only be entitled to some money back if repeated downloads failed to resolve the problem and you could demonstrate that the problem was not incompatibility with your device or music player.

⇨ The above information is reprinted with kind permission from the Department for Business Innovation & Skills. Please visit discuss.bis.gov.uk for further information.

Protect yourself

Advice from the Financial Conduct Authority.

Financial services firms can only operate in the UK if they are authorised by us or registered to do so, or are otherwise exempt.

Unfortunately, there are firms in the UK and abroad that operate without our authorisation, and some knowingly run scams.

Protect yourself from unauthorised firms

Follow our ten steps to make sure you are dealing with an authorised firm, and to protect yourself from fraud and unauthorised activity.

Firms and individuals can only conduct regulated financial services activities in the UK if they are authorised by us or registered to do so, or are otherwise exempt. Yet some act without our authorisation or knowingly run scams.

If you deal with an unauthorised firm you will not be covered by the Financial Ombudsman Service (FOS) or Financial Services Compensation Scheme (FSCS) if things go wrong.

But there are steps you can take to make sure you are dealing with an authorised firm, and to protect yourself from fraud and unauthorised activity.

Ten steps to avoid unauthorised firms

Step 1: Check the Register

We strongly advise you to only deal with financial services firms that are authorised by us or registered, and check the Register to ensure they are.

The Register has information on firms and individuals that are, or have been, regulated by us.

If a firm does not appear on the Register but claims it does, contact our Consumer Helpline on 0800 111 6768.

Step 2: Ring them back

To confirm the identity of an authorised firm on the Register, ask for their 'firm reference number' (FRN) and contact details, but always call them back on the switchboard number given on the Register rather than a direct line they might give you.

If there are no contact details on the Register or the firm claims they are out of date, contact our Consumer Helpline on 0800 111 6768.

Step 3: Use the right website

You should access the Register from our website – www.fca.org.uk – rather than through links in e-mails or on the website of a firm offering you an investment.

Also check the address of our website is correct and there are not subtle changes that mean it is a fake.

Step 4: Beware of cloned firms

You should also beware of fraudsters pretending to be from a firm authorised by us, as it could be what we call a 'cloned firm'.

These scammers often claim to be from overseas firms that appear on the Register as these firms do not always have their full contact and website details listed.

Step 5: Make additional checks

With fraudsters adapting their tactics you should make additional checks to confirm you are dealing with the financial services firm in question and have the correct contact details – especially if you have been cold-called.

You might want to check the details on the firm's website, with directory enquiries or Companies House.

Step 6: Check if a firm is authorised or registered

Almost all financial services firms and individuals must be authorised by us. But certain types of firms may instead be registered with us, including some payment services providers and electronic money (e-money) institutions, mutual societies like credit unions, friendly societies, cooperative societies, working men's clubs and building societies.

You can check the Register to see whether a firm is authorised by us or registered.

Beware that registered firms do not have to provide us with as much detail about their business and we have less power to check on the firm

You can contact our Consumer Helpline on 0800 111 6768 if you have any problems or questions about using the Register or what the information in it means.

Step 7: Search our list of unauthorised firms

You can look through our list of unauthorised firms to avoid doing business with, although their names are likely to change regularly. This is a list of firms and individuals that are currently targeting UK investors and we have received complaints about.

We add new names to this list as soon as possible, but if the firm which has approached you does not appear on our list, do not assume it is legitimate – it may not have been reported to us yet.

Step 8: See warnings from abroad

If you are dealing with an overseas firm or scheme you should check how it is regulated and follow similar steps to these.

We also have some warnings from foreign regulators about firms conducting unauthorised business.

Step 9: Avoid unwanted sales calls

Keep in mind that authorised firms that you have no relationship with are highly unlikely to contact you out of the blue.

You can also reduce the number of unsolicited mailings and cold calls you receive by registering with the Telephone Preference Service and Mailing Preference Service.

Step 10: Report an unauthorised firm

If you think you have been approached by an unauthorised firm you should contact our Consumer Helpline on 0800 111 6768.

We also have reporting forms that you can use to tell us about an unauthorised firm or broker involved in certain business areas, such as consumer credit, mortgages, insurance products, payment services and share fraud.

Misleading adverts

Find out the difference between clear and misleading financial advertising, and what to do when you think an advert is misleading.

Financial advertising and promotions should clearly explain what the product or service is, how it works and how you could benefit from it. It must also be clear about the costs involved and whether there are any risks to your money.

However, some financial adverts are not clear and fair, and we find some are misleading.

How to spot a misleading advert

Financial adverts and promotions can be misleading for many reasons, but there are some questions you can consider to help you spot and avoid misleading adverts, such as:

⇨ Do I have to pay a fee?

⇨ What are the interest rates and when will interest be paid?

⇨ Are the interest rates or returns being promoted realistic?

⇨ What are the risks to my money and is this clear?

⇨ How long do I have to commit for?

⇨ Are there any penalties if I want to move my money?

⇨ Is the product guaranteed and how does it work?

⇨ Are there important points that are only shown in the small print?

Report a misleading advert

We can look at adverts and promotions relating to most financial products and service, including banking and savings, investments and advice, insurance, mortgages, pensions, and loan and credit products.

If you think a financial advert or promotion is unfair or unclear, you can report a misleading advert to us.

When we find that an advert is misleading we can:

⇨ ask the firm to change or remove the advert

⇨ ask the firm to write to customers who may have been misled and compensate them if they have lost money as a result

⇨ warn or fine the firm.

Please note that we usually cannot discuss our investigations or findings with you, but we appreciate you helping us to protect consumers and firms from misleading adverts.

Who else to contact

If you want to complain about more general parts of an advert or promotion, such as over the taste and decency or social responsibility, contact the Advertising Standards Authority (ASA).

Please be aware that we can not resolve individual disputes you have with a firm or arrange compensation. If you are unhappy with a financial product or service you should find out how to complain.

12 September 2014

⇨ The above information is reprinted with kind permission from the Financial Conduct Authority. Please visit www.fca. org.uk for further information.

© FCA 2014

Should Sunday trading restrictions be relaxed?

The Sunday Trading Act that came into force 20 years ago this month ended years of wrangling over whether retailers should open seven days a week.

By Rebecca Thomson

But while the final decision, which allowed stores over 3,000 sq ft to open for six hours, was the compromise settled on at the time, is it still enough in a world where shoppers expect to be able to order online 24/7, and where shopping experiences are built around convenience?

Some retailers don't think so. Asda, Selfridges and Morrisons have all come out in favour of a review of Sunday hours.

An Asda spokesman says: 'Our customers' shopping habits have changed significantly in recent years with convenience ranking high, alongside value. Retailers need to adapt to meet the needs of customers, which is why we support a review of Sunday trading laws.'

Ann Summers chief executive Jacqueline Gold says the law is too restrictive. 'We need Sunday trading hours to be more reflective of the society we live in today. Consumers want access to retailers when it suits them and the reality is being open 11am to 5pm on a Sunday just doesn't work.'

She points out that allowing shops to open on a Sunday doesn't mean the day will become totally focused on shopping.

'Most families will want to spend a Sunday together, but there may also be a need to pop to the shops too,' she says.

'Forcing people to do this in the middle of the day means that Sundays become less flexible. I know that for me Sundays are about being with my daughter and husband, but if I need to get to a shop then I would much rather get this done at 9am.'

Longer hours

An exclusive ICM poll of shoppers for *Retail Week* – see right – found that more than half of consumers (51%) believe further relaxation of the laws would benefit high streets as they emerge from the downturn.

And just under half (48%) think large shops such as supermarkets should be allowed to open longer on Sundays.

The debate over Sunday trading hours raised its head again earlier this year, with a Parliamentary bid to extend trading hours led by Conservative MP Philip Davies.

He said in April: 'I would like to scrap the Sunday trading restrictions altogether. The sky has not fallen in Scotland where there are no such rules. If people want to keep Sunday special that is fine, they can do so. It is about freedom of choice.'

The new high streets minister, Penny Mordaunt, also thinks the issue needs to be explored. She told *Retail Week*: 'I think we have seen shopping evolve and change. People have different demands now.

'We've got to explore these issues and of course need to be aware that employees, particularly those working part time, will feel they have less family time. But I think there are ways to get round it in terms of how large businesses arrange the rotas.'

In addition, 35% of shoppers polled by ICM say longer opening hours on a Sunday would make things easier for them, with many wanting to 'get things done' on a Sunday.

But while the issue used to polarise retailers, splitting the industry starkly down the middle, the attitude today is slightly more lackadaisical.

While some, such as Selfridges chief executive Paul Kelly, are staunchly in favour, others such as Sainsbury's and Tesco are less worried. While many retailers want more flexibility, others say longer Sunday hours wouldn't result in extra sales but instead spread them across the weekend.

Good compromise

Sainsbury's has been relaxed about the situation for the past few years. A spokeswoman says: 'Our position on Sunday trading is that we think the current situation is a good compromise. Our customers haven't asked us for longer supermarket trading hours.'

This current position echoes the sentiment of former chief executive Justin King, who said in a letter to the *Daily Telegraph* in 2012 that extending Sunday hours is not the 'magic answer' to solving the UK's economic problems. He said: 'Maintaining Sunday's special status has great merit.'

Tesco is also relaxed about the need for reform. A spokesman for the grocer says: 'We understand there are strong views on either side of the debate over further liberalisation of Sunday trading. Whilst we recognise the benefits on a limited basis, such as the Olympics in 2012, we are mindful of the impact this would have on our colleagues. We do not have any plans to change our current position.'

Some consumers are unsure about shopping on a Sunday as well. While 41% shop frequently on a Sunday, the ICM poll shows, 42% say they shop 'less frequently' on a Sunday. Supermarkets are the most popular choice, with 71% of shoppers using them on a Sunday.

In addition, 26% of shoppers surveyed say they don't believe shops should be open at all on a Sunday – a surprisingly high figure in an environment where convenience and 24-hour shopping is assumed to be what every shopper wants.

Kate Bewick, associate director at ICM, says the responses from shoppers differ according to age. Those over 45 are more likely to look askance the idea of Sunday trading than the under-45s, who have grown up accustomed to it and accept it as normal.

On the fence

'There's not necessarily wholehearted support or disagreement,' she says. 'People are on the fence – a substantial proportion of people support further reform but it's not a majority and it's certainly not overwhelming.'

But one thing that most do seem to agree on is that longer trading hours would probably provide a boost to high streets, especially those that are struggling.

The ICM poll found 51% of respondents say longer opening hours on a Sunday would bring more people on to the high street, which would be good for all retailers there.

The Open Sundays campaign is pushing for reform on Sunday trading, and the group argues longer trading hours would increase retail spending and help retailers become more of a leisure destination for people looking for things to do on a Sunday.

Open Sundays' director Mark Allatt says: 'Our high streets need to be able to better compete with online retailers that are able to sell 24/7 with no restrictions.'

Sunday trading has always been an emotive issue for retailers – and 20 years on, the debate over the right opening hours is still not quite resolved.

1 August 2014

⇨ The above information is reprinted with kind permission from *Retail Week*. Please visit www.retail-week.com for further information.

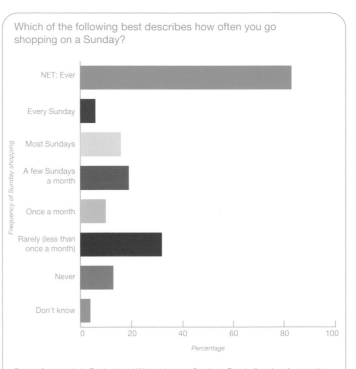

Which of the following best describes how often you go shopping on a Sunday?

Four in five people in England and Wales shop on Sundays. Two in five shop frequently on Sundays (more than once a month), and two in five go less often. Just over one in ten consumers (13%) say they never go shopping on Sundays. Less affluent consumers (DE) are less likely than other social grades to shop frequently on a Sunday (32%).There are some indicative differences by region with the South East seeing the highest proportion of those shopping frequently on a Sunday (47%)

Source: ICM Research on behalf of Retail Week (July/August 2014)

Public views on ethical retail

Public opinion research conducted by Ipsos MORI on behalf of the Department for Business, Innovation and Skills, 2014.

Introduction and methodology

The Department for Business, Innovation and Skills commissioned Ipsos MORI to conduct a survey into UK attitudes to ethical standards in retail and their impact on the public's buying decisions.

Research was conducted on i:omnibus, Ipsos MORI's online omnibus, among a total of 2,257 adults aged 16+ in the United Kingdom, between 13 and 17 June 2014

Survey data were weighted by age, gender, region, social grade, working status and main shopper to the known population profile to be nationally representative of adults aged 16+ in the UK.

Main findings

⇨ Half (49%) of UK adults aged 16 or over believe that, in general, retail companies are 'not very' or 'not at all' ethical nowadays ('ethical' is defined as selling products that are ethically produced and following good principles in their behaviour and decisions). By contrast, just under two in five (37%) believe retailers are 'fairly' or 'very ethical' nowadays.

• Men are more likely than women to say that retail companies are 'not at all ethical'; 12% of men feel this way compared to 8% of women.

• 16–24-year-olds have a more positive view of the ethical standards of retailers than some older age groups. Just under half (46%) think companies are 'fairly ethical', compared to three in ten (30%) 25–34-year-olds, just under one in three 35–44 and 55–75-year-olds (32% each) and just under two in five of those aged 45–54-years-old or over 75 (37% each).

• Social grade also has an influence on perceptions of ethics in retail; just under half of AB (45%) and C1 (44%) social grades say that retailers are 'not very ethical' compared to around one in three in the C2 (35%) and DE (32%) bands.

⇨ Overall, the ethical standards of retail companies and the products they sell is an issue that matters at least a little to more than four in five adults (83%). For half (49%) it matters 'a great deal' or 'a fair amount'.

• Ethical standards of retailers and their products matter more to women than to men; women are more likely to say this 'matters a fair amount' (38%) than men (31%). Men are more likely to say retail companies' ethical standards 'do not matter at all' to them (14%) than women (6%).

⇨ Just under two in five (39%) UK adults say that they have made a buying decision that

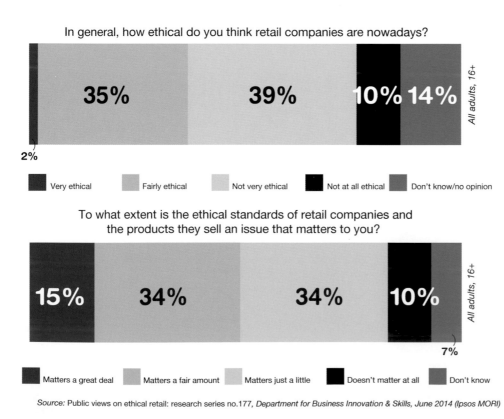

In general, how ethical do you think retail companies are nowadays?

35%   39%   10% 14%

All adults, 16+

2%

■ Very ethical   ■ Fairly ethical   ■ Not very ethical   ■ Not at all ethical   ■ Don't know/no opinion

To what extent is the ethical standards of retail companies and the products they sell an issue that matters to you?

15%   34%   34%   10%

All adults, 16+

7%

■ Matters a great deal   ■ Matters a fair amount   ■ Matters just a little   ■ Doesn't matter at all   ■ Don't know

Source: Public views on ethical retail: research series no.177, Department for Business Innovation & Skills, June 2014 (Ipsos MORI)

was influenced by the ethical standards of a retailer or product in the last year. However, over a quarter (28%) say their buying decisions have never been influenced in this way and a similar proportion (26%) don't know or can't say if they have taken this into consideration.

- Men are more likely than women to say they have never made a buying decision that was influenced in this way (33% vs 24%), while women are more likely to say they don't know or can't say (31% of women vs 22% of men).

⇨ Just under two in five (38%) agree that they try to buy products from companies that act in an ethical way, even if it means spending more, while one in five (22%) disagree.

- Women are more likely than men to agree with this proposition (42% of women vs 33% of men). Those aged 25–34 are less likely than other age groups to agree (30%).

⇨ Just under two in three (63%) agree that it is not sufficient for companies to tell them that they are ethical, but need to prove this is the case.

- Women are more likely than men to agree that companies should prove that they are ethical (44% vs 36%).

⇨ A similar proportion (62%) agree that it is important that retail companies are clear about where they source their raw materials, components or ingredients from.

- Again, women are more likely than men to agree: just under half of women agree (46%) compared to just over one in three men (36%).

⇨ Pricing is the main factor that makes people less likely to buy products produced in an ethical way. Just under two

Which of the following reasons, if any, make you less likely to buy products that are produced in an ethical way?

Base: adults aged 16+ in the UK (2,257) 13–17 June 2014

39%
Ethical products tend to have higher prices

33%
Information about ethical products isn't easily available

30%
Ethical options aren't well advertised

11%
My preferred brands don't offer ethical options

12%
I'm not concerned about whether products are produced in an ethical way

24%
Information about ethical products isn't reliable

5%
Ethical products tend to be lower quality

7%
None of the above

15%
Don't know

Source: Public views on ethical retail: research series no.177, Department for Business Innovation & Skills, June 2014 (Ipsos MORI)

fifths (39%) say a belief that ethical products tend to have higher prices makes them less likely to buy these goods.

- This is more of an issue for women (43%) than for men (36%). Those aged 55–75 are the least likely to see this as an issue (30% say prices make them less likely to buy ethical products).

- For one in three (33%), a lack of easily available information about ethical products is a barrier to purchase.

- Again, women are more likely than men to cite this reason (36% vs 30%). Those over 75 are more likely to see a lack of information as an issue than 16–24-year-olds; over two in five (43%) over-75s compared to a quarter (25%) of 16–24-year-olds.

⇨ Three in ten (30%) say they are less likely to buy ethical

options because they aren't well advertised. A further one in four (24%) are less likely to do so because they believe information about ethical goods isn't reliable. The latter is a particular issue for those over 75, where just under two in five (38%) see this as a reason not to buy ethical products.

⇨ Just 5% say they are less likely to buy ethical products through a belief that they tend to be lower quality.

- A little more than one in ten (12%) say they are not concerned about whether products are produced in an ethical way.

June 2014

⇨ The above information is reprinted with kind permission from the Department for Business Innovation & Skills. Please visit discuss.bis. gov.uk for further information.

© Crown copyright 2014

Ethical Consumer Markets Report 2013

Ethical markets in the UK continue to show strong growth despite recessionary pressures.

Latest figures show that sales of ethical products grew by more than 12% in a year when the UK economy grew by only 0.2%. The ethical market is now worth just over £54 billion – greater than the market for alcohol and tobacco.

This report shows how governments, companies, consumers and campaigners have all played a role in driving this growth.

'The impact of ethical consumer behaviours around food and drink increased by 36% in 2012 to reach £10.16 billion'

Significant contributions include:

⇨ Sales of Rainforest Alliance certified food products up by 47% with big companies making these products more widely available

⇨ Spending on micro-generation (renewables) up by 50% continuing to benefit from generous government incentives

⇨ Sales of A-rates cars (a CO_2 emission ranking) soaring by 157% amidst higher costs of fuel, government incentives and a wider choice of models from manufacturers.

According to Rob Harrison, a Director at Ethical Consumer Research Association, 'The annual *Ethical Consumer Markets Reports* have shown significant growth each year since the onset of the recession. This clearly demonstrates that the trend towards ethical buying is not a luxury which consumers choose to drop when the going gets tough, but an important long-term change in the way people are making buying decisions.'

Not every sector is growing though, and there were small falls in some sectors where price issues are most challenging. These include organic food (down by 4%) and ethical clothing (down by 1%).

And the trend towards ethical purchasing is also moving outwards into new product areas. This year ethical jewellery and 'co-consumption' have been added to the barometer, as some reliable new datasets become available. Fairtrade certified gold, for example, is now making an impact in the jewellery sector. And 'co-consumption' – where people get together to share items rather than purchasing them outright – now has some high-profile players such as London's 'Boris Bikes' cycle hire scheme.

'Sales of green home products were up by 7% to £8.9 billion'

Although ethical markets are still a small proportion of overall spending it is possible to observe how, in some markets where ethical purchasing has been going on for a long time – such as eggs, coffee and bananas – a dominant market share for ethical products is on the horizon. The trends in this year's Report continue to show how this remains a realistic long-term possibility for most UK consumer markets.

Key findings
Ethical food and drink

The impact of ethical consumer behaviours around food and drink increased by 36% in 2012 to reach £10.16 billion. Big movers were Rainforest Alliance products (such as tea and coffee) certified for

Ethical food and drink	2010 £million	2011 £million	2012 £million	% growth 2011–2012
Organic food	1,475	1,382	1,332	-4%
Fairtrade	1,064	1,253	1,552	24%
Rainforest Alliance	1,197	1,345	1,980	47%
Free-range eggs	419	525	577	10%
Free-range poultry	251	265	261	-2%
Vegetarian meat alternatives	541	573	613	7%
Freedom food	572	740	1,012	37%
Sustainable fish	141	293	353	20%
Boycotts total	1,084	1,113	2,478	123%
Total	**6,744**	**7,489**	**10,158**	**36%**

minimum environmental and human rights standards. They saw sales increase by 46%. Also growing fast was the RSPCA's Freedom Foods label with total sales up by 37%. Less strong in the year were organic food (down 4%) and free-range poultry (down 2%).

Green home

Sales of green home products, including energy efficient white goods, sustainable timber and renewable energy installations, were up by 7% to £8.9 billion. Although the highest feed-in-tariff rates were only available for three months during this period, home solar panel installations were so popular that sales grew by 50% over the previous year. Green energy sales were down 171%. This was because most of the big electricity companies abandoned their green electricity tariffs during this period following regulatory changes forcing them to simplify their pricing structures. However, smaller green electricity players all saw growth.

Eco-travel and transport

Economic activity in ethical travel and transport increased by 46% to £4.5 billion. The biggest mover was sales of electric, hybrid and tax band A efficient vehicles which were up by 157% as a result of many more models becoming available in this area.

Ethical personal products

Sales of ethical personal products were relatively static, rising by only 3% to £1.8 billion. There was a big rise in the purchase of second-hand clothing (31% up) and a fall in the sales (1% down) of specialist ethical clothing. This fits with the story of straitened budgets in recessionary times.

New entrants in the personal products sector were ethical jewellery with £3.6 million of sales and co-consumption with £10.4 million.

⇨ The above information is reprinted with kind permission from the Ethical Consumer Research Association. Please visit www.ethicalconsumer.org for further information.

To what degree do ethics play a role in consumers' purchasing decisions?

By Michael Jary

Tesco and Sainsbury's recent dispute over whether Fairtrade products can be price-compared with non-Fairtrade comes down to what degree ethics play a role in consumers' purchasing decisions. There is a strong body of evidence suggesting that the Fairtrade mark enhances consumer preference and loyalty, meaning fair trade makes commercial as well as ethical sense for retailers.

Ethical marks are no longer just for the affluent, they have broken into the mainstream. Duchy Originals, an early pioneer in the organic movement, is celebrating its 21st birthday, and next year Fairtrade celebrates its 20th. Both began as ambitious projects that many said were foolhardy. Over two decades, their success can be measured not only by their growth but by the proliferation of ethical brands and certification standards that have emerged in their wake. To some degree this has cannibalised the organic sector (although Duchy Originals from Waitrose has pulled ahead in share). Consumers can now choose between an increasing selection of ethical labels such as free range, Red Tractor or Freedom Food. But overall the ethical sector is larger, more vibrant and more hotly competed than ever.

Extreme poverty, climate change, environmental depletion, human rights abuses, poor animal welfare and food security are just some of the profound challenges faced by the global consumer goods system. As the ethical sector moves into the mainstream, there is a realisation that it can scale up to contribute to the solution. However, two elements remain important: becoming more transparent and striving for even greater impact. Transparency is critical, enabling an increasingly informed consumer to explore the consequences of their choices,

and empowering the producer to evaluate the benefits of sustainable development. The Fairtrade Foundation has participated in the creation of AskMalawi.tv, a website that connects the consumer directly with a Malawian farmer group. These farmers are armed with mobile video cameras to answer questions about what life is really like in a rural farming community. Consumers don't have to take the retailer's or even Fairtrade's word for the difference they can make, they can find out for themselves.

Continuous improvement is also essential. The realities of dealing with complex supply chain systems while striving for the right ethical outcomes are rarely straightforward. This is why Duchy Originals from Waitrose and the Prince of Wales's Charitable Foundation support the Duchy Originals Future Farming Programme, helping British farmers to find ways to improve yield and productivity while continuing to farm in an environmentally friendly way.

Internationally, it is why Fairtrade not only insists that producers must meet standards on child labour, but works with farms and their communities to address the root causes of the problem through raising incomes and improving real conditions for children.

The next phase of ethical and sustainable business will take us towards new models.

But scaling up into the mainstream is now unstoppable: this is no longer a niche sector.

29 August 2013

⇨ The above information is reprinted with kind permission from *Retail Week*. Please visit www.retail-week.com for further information.

How much do consumers really care about transparency?

The Guardian's *experts shared their views on how consumers perceive transparency in business and what motivates them to buy or discard, endorse or avoid.*

By Sarah LaBrecque

What does transparency mean to consumers today?

As concerns over value chain management continue to make news, it seems only a matter of time before the next supply chain scandal strikes the fear of horsemeat into our hearts. Questions around transparency have never seemed more pertinent, but has the concept taken on new meaning in the wake of repeated embarrassments?

Ashish Deo, director of commercial relations at Fairtrade Foundation, says: 'Transparency is really an expansion of the idea of quality, as markets and consumers have evolved. So while quality may have meant more specific things regarding physical products earlier, we now include many other dimensions such as responsibility and sustainability.'

Transparency is no longer about how well made a product is or even whether it is certified organic, but about how and where the materials in the product were sourced. If a jumper is Fairtrade, for example, does it nevertheless contain angora from China?

Consumers equate transparency with a full roster of social, environmental and labour standards – which they expect to be able to get their hands on to read for themselves. But do they also, perhaps naively, expect that governments will have checks in place to ensure this level of accountability?

Safia Minney, founder and chief executive of sustainable fashion retailer People Tree, says an 'ethical policy'

on a website which is little more than greenwash doesn't cut it any more. 'Consumers expect that their governments are setting decent standards for good business practice overseas, but sadly this is not the case,' she says.

Do consumers really care about these issues, and are they willing to pay more for a 'sustainable' product?

Some of the panellists agreed that consumers are apathetic when it comes to investigating deep into a company's supply chain. It might be a task even to figure out what 'FSC' certified means. Ryan D. Jacobs, general manager at Ten Thousand Villages Canada, explains: 'I think labels become a crutch that allow people to feel better about their purchases, but rarely do they understand what's behind them.'

And Britons are less willing than the global average to spend more for a brand which they believe to be acting ethically. Rob Myers, a managing director at pollsters Ipsos MORI, offered some interesting statistics: 'Only 39% of UK consumers say they would "buy products from brands that act responsibly, even if it means spending more". Globally the average is 54%.'

So even though the word 'transparency' has taken on new meanings, consumers still won't necessarily shell out in response. If consumers are concerned, are they concerned enough?

Martyn Leadbeater, sales director at logistics company Advanced Supply Chain, says people have historically been more worried about the environmental impact of products, but that social concerns have had more influence in consumer's minds in recent times.

Is hyper-transparency advisable for businesses?

How much is too much? Can hyper-transparency work for all products and supply chains or are there reasons for companies to hold back?

As part of its overall ethical policy, Fairphone has published a complete cost breakdown of its €350 phone saying it wants to account for every Euro that has gone into it. And Starbucks' environmental impact director Jim Hanna has proclaimed that hyper-transparency is something that the coffee chain welcomes.

Jacobs is pragmatic. 'I think it might work for certain commodities or tangible products like a phone – so in principle, it makes sense. But there's a lot of context that isn't captured in such details,' he says.

And it won't always translate into improved consumer trust. Myers believes that it might be effective for some, but consumers already have too much product information to contend with. Deo believes it is futile to zero in on the consumer at all. 'This is really about businesses fulfilling their responsibilities,' he says. 'Economic transparency at business level is a key requirement for fostering the right kind of collaboration.'

So while hyper-transparency might be appropriate for some businesses, it won't necessarily help to improve customer relations; the average shopper is not invested in that level of detail.

Karen Hetherington, systems director at Fullwell Mill, which manufactures organic, Fairtrade and healthy foods, feels systems should be in place to track and gather important information about partners and stakeholders. This is an alternative to overburdening the consumer with too much detail and the business with added costs.

Transparency in business is a means to an end, not the end in and of itself, according to Lisa Hoyle, technical director for group food sourcing at Tesco. 'Done well, it can create the space for collaboration, innovation and efficiency and most importantly, it can help customers make the right choices,' she concludes.

12 March 2014

⇨ The above information is reprinted with kind permission from *The Guardian*. Please visit www.theguardian.com for further information.

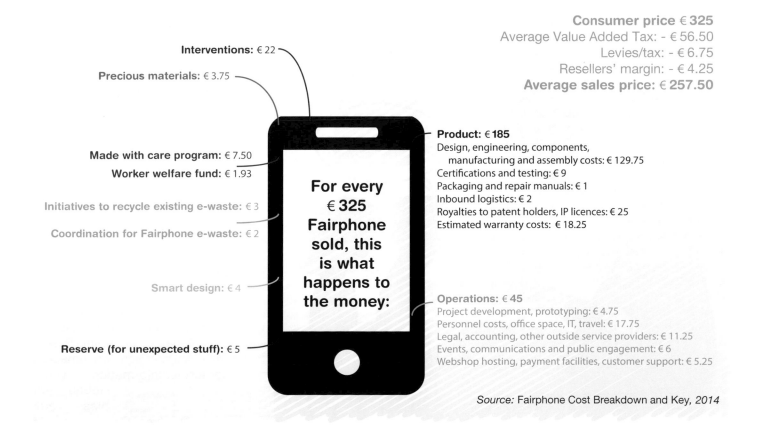

Consumer price € 325
Average Value Added Tax: - € 56.50
Levies/tax: - € 6.75
Resellers' margin: - € 4.25
Average sales price: € 257.50

Interventions: € 22
Precious materials: € 3.75

Made with care program: € 7.50
Worker welfare fund: € 1.93
Initiatives to recycle existing e-waste: € 3
Coordination for Fairphone e-waste: € 2
Smart design: € 4
Reserve (for unexpected stuff): € 5

For every € 325 Fairphone sold, this is what happens to the money:

Product: € 185
Design, engineering, components, manufacturing and assembly costs: € 129.75
Certifications and testing: € 9
Packaging and repair manuals: € 1
Inbound logistics: € 2
Royalties to patent holders, IP licences: € 25
Estimated warranty costs: € 18.25

Operations: € 45
Project development, prototyping: € 4.75
Personnel costs, office space, IT, travel: € 17.75
Legal, accounting, other outside service providers: € 11.25
Events, communications and public engagement: € 6
Webshop hosting, payment facilities, customer support: € 5.25

Source: Fairphone Cost Breakdown and Key, *2014*

opportunities offered by such new technology.

In a report subtitled *Understanding the changing consumer*, Accenture observes, 'Consumers are increasingly "connected" – often online, interacting with companies and other consumers to research and purchase products, share advice, and praise or criticize a business. Nearly three-quarters of the consumers surveyed said they use the Internet to research or purchase products or services more than they did three years ago. Consumers are also increasingly using social media as a tool in the purchasing process.'

Reflecting that directly on the high street itself, however, is a challenge for brands and consumers. Brent Hoberman, the co-founder of lastminute.com and now of online furniture retailer made.com, argues that technology can strengthen both aspects.

'In the near future we're going to see an awful lot of visualisation technology,' he says. 'Returns with sofas were often because people couldn't fit it through the door, but we're going to see people uploading floorplans of their houses so that we know how everything will fit in. And augmented reality means that we will be able to see what items will look like in place, too.'

But even made.com has a showroom. 'It's currently on the 9th floor in Notting Hill Gate,' says Hoberman, 'and it's a very small percentage of shoppers who visit it. But there's something reassuring for customers knowing we have a physical presence.' Hoberman says that he thinks high street outlets will essentially be advertising for a brand, which will then allow users to shop online in store. 'Big shops will become sort of brand cathedrals,' he argues.

For the high street itself, that means small shops partnering with larger suppliers, so that they can tailor what is offered to very local areas but benefit from the global market. 'A combination of more flexible retail spaces, short lets and partnerships will mean in

some senses the high street will be more connected but look more local,' he says.

Making the Internet tangible is a challenge that some companies are meeting simply by building gadgets. In South Korea, for instance, takeaway food suppliers have launched a button, wirelessly connected to a user's phone, that people can stick on their fridge. Press it and your favourite takeaway automatically delivers your favourite pizza. Little matter that it could just be a button on a smartphone screen.

With so many possibilities, however, people who are actually building the high street of the future have to make some big bets. At the Battersea Power Station development, opening from 2016 but not finished until 2024, the developers must plan what they think shoppers will actually want.

'It's clear that as online shopping has grown in popularity so planners, developers and retailers are going to have to work harder and harder to bring people into town centres and retail developments,' says

Rob Tincknell, Battersea's Chief Executive.

'High street shopping needs to evolve so visitors are offered not just a variety of shops, but also a variety of recreational opportunities. That means shops, cafes, galleries and restaurants side by side and framed with architecture and landscaping that make it a stimulating and rewarding place to visit.'

And anyway, says Tincknell, 'showrooming' is here to stay: 'Shops themselves will need to evolve to serve a generation of customers who may well want to visit a shop in order to experience the product – but will ultimately transact online.'

24 January 2013

⇨ The above information is reprinted with kind permission from *The Telegraph*. Please visit www.telegraph.co.uk for further information.

Future of British high streets will see fewer retailers, more services and better community activities

By Charlie Thomas

Since the beginning of the recession, a high number of retail casualties have resulted in empty buildings filling up our high streets.

In 2008, Woolworths was the first of the big names to fall, and many smaller chains suffered after that. Jane Norman, Kookai, Barratts, Peacocks, Threshers, Clinton Cards, Birthdays, Sony Centres, among many others followed Woolworths into administration.

In the past month, Comet, Jessops, HMV and Blockbuster have all joined them – so what next for our ailing high street? Many readers have written to the Huffington Post UK upset at their local community becoming full of fast food eateries, betting shops, pound stores and charity shops where once there was a vibrant atmosphere. Is this the future for the UK's town centres?

The end of the retail era

Perhaps the biggest shift for which most town planners are preparing is a shift away from a retail focus for our high streets.

Retail guru Mary Portas wrote a report into the future of British high streets for the Government's consideration in 2011, and while its suggestions were solid for shop owners, the report received criticism for being too focused on retail being the saviour of our high streets.

From this year, many are predicting a rise in other services on our high streets; diagnostic medical centres, police services in our post offices, libraries acting as community centres for all manner of purposes – this will be the year where the high street stops being all about shopping and becomes more about a sense of community.

Indeed, the Royal Town Planning Institute entered its views for the Future of London's town centres call for evidence earlier this month and noted: 'Town centres should look to be renewed via the development of what the commission terms "lifetime neighbourhoods" – e.g. that town centres become the main locations for delivery of public as well as private services such as education, health, civic, voluntary...'

Josef Hargrave, a member of Arup's foresight and innovation team, told the Huffington Post UK: 'There needs to be a move away from thinking high streets are just for shopping. There's already talk about a bit of a shift of understanding, whereby the high street becomes a community centre.

'Future gazing workshops on the NHS are already discussing having community diagnosis centres for non-serious medical concerns, particularly with an ageing population on the horizon.'

David Jeevendrampillai, part of a team at UCL which looks at building Adaptable Suburbs, agrees. Trained as an anthropologist, Jeevendrampillai studies the importance of developing a purpose for the high street and the wider community as a whole.

'People want a healthy, vibrant local economy, but what we're seeing is that lots of those sorts of businesses are already further away from the high street. Most small businesses are run from the home and built on networks of trust that go beyond the physical nature of the high street,' he said.

'Lots of businesses operate out of their homes, but there's a big gap to get them onto the high street. A lot of good work is being done by unpaid community volunteers to bring creative, vibrant atmospheres back to our towns. Most of these volunteers don't even own local businesses; they just want their area to be a nice place to live. Councils should take more notice of them, instead of sitting in static meetings.'

There is also evidence to suggest that good planning for bringing public services into town centres could have positive effects on mental health and well-being of individuals, as well as promoting community cohesion.

Councils are often asked to help do their bit by encouraging affordable rents and offering sustainable town planning – but in a market where a fast buck wins over long-term investment this could be hard.

'Those high streets that are full of pound shops and kebab houses are down to bad planning', said Hargrave. 'It's hard though. Once you're on a downward spiral of only granting licences to those stores it needs a big intervention to turn an area around, and that means a lot of capital investment.

A nostalgic idea? Or a myth?

UCL's Professor Laura Vaughan told the Huffington Post UK that she believed the current call for the death of the high street was based on an idea of a high street which for many never really existed.

'We've been studying four outer London cases from the 1860s onwards and find that change and continuity are both part of the story of town centres,' she explained.

'Every generation comes out with a statement forecasting the "death" of the high street and is proven to be wrong. We no longer visit the high street on foot to shop at the butcher, the baker and the candlestick maker, but we do still make local trips on foot, bicycle and car to the post office, library, greengrocer, nursery, bike repair shop and so on.'

What makes some high streets able to survive while others are less resilient is less well understood, but there are similarities which these towns have.

Towns that survive are not dependent solely on local people coming in every day to visit the shops; they are situated within a network that feeds movement through and to the locations, and that movement isn't driven by just shopping, but also work, commuting to get elsewhere, education establishments, leisure facilities and so on.

So, is retail dead?

No. Far from it in fact, but it does need to adapt to stay alive, and to encourage shoppers back to the high street.

Making the stores efficient is key. Arup's Hargrave pointed to Regent Street in London as an example of improved efficiency leading to a vibrant shopping area. The Crown Estate recognised that there was too much traffic running along and stopping along Regent Street, and so it called on all of the shops to share one logistics fleet.

Now, all of the excess stock is kept in Enfield, and deliveries come through one lorry that serves the whole street. This has two positive effects – the streets aren't constantly blocked with lorries – in fact deliveries have been reduced by 80% as a result – and secondly the store-owners get more space in their buildings freed up, as there's no need to store extra stock on site. This means the shopping experience is improved for the customer, enticing them to come back.

Outside of efficiencies, Hargrave recommends improving the in-store experience by, for example, offering goods and services that don't appear online.

'Selfridges' "No Noise" zone is a nice innovation; granted it's not something everyone has the space to do, but it provides a nice experience for the customer,' he said.

Stores should embrace technology too – the forward thinking retailers are creating 'living labs' where the physical stores have sensors to record how customers behave.

For clothing retailers for example, sensors can detect which items are paired with others, which could give you a heads up on how customers would like to see items displayed. Data on how long customers spend in each section of your store can also be analysed to provide a better customer experience.

And in a futuristic twist, telecoms giant Telefonica is beginning to take data from its mobile customers' data usage and planning to sell the information along to retailers to help them personalise their stores to coincide with the type of person who's walking past them.

'If you know that at 4pm a high number of older ladies pass your shop on their way to or from something, you could offer something in the window which appeals to that demographic,' Hargrave explained.

'Or if you know a bunch of builders are working on a site around the corner, if you're in food retail you could put on a "builders' special" of bacon butties and tea for when they're on the way to work.' By using this data, physical stores can compete with the online ecosystem.

The future?

Fast forward to 2023 and beyond, and what could our high streets

feature? Again, technology leads the way – and for Josef Hargrave, innovations like 3D printing could be used to great effect on the high street, especially for retailers.

'Just imagine, you walk into a store, get your body scanned, and get tailor-made clothing designed to fit you exactly using a 3D printer – that's something you'd go to the high street for,' he said.

Richard Coleman, director of SME at Zurich worked alongside best-selling science-fiction writer Alastair Reynolds at a recent event for SMEs.

From the workshops they ran he suggests the high streets will exist in both physical and digital spaces at the same time, a sort of hybrid high street.

'An SME operating without a fixed location could rent an empty property on a street which it then fills with virtual products and services,' he offered.

'However, in the far future, SMEs could look to share retail space: if the shop staff and contents are virtual, then multiple shop occupancies could happen at the same time.

'This may mean that customers could walk into almost any kind of store, depending on their augmented reality preferences. There could be a 100 customers in the empty shop at one time, all experiencing different consumer environments.'

19 January 2013

Hard-to-please 'fauxsumers' pin it and save it but rarely buy it

An article from The Conversation.

By Shailey Minocha, Reader in Computing at The Open University

THE CONVERSATION

Ever since there were shops, people have enjoyed window shopping. But a new phenomenon is emerging that takes the habit to the extreme.

If you save things to your Amazon wishlist without ever actually buying them, browse gadgets, clothes and offers online as a pastime or fill your shopping cart without going through with the payment, you may be a fauxsumer.

This 'false consumerism', particularly prevalent among millennials, is the process of discovering products online without purchasing anything. Shopping without having the goal of actually buying.

The rise of fauxsumerism was revealed in a recent study of 1,300 14- to 34-year-olds in the US. These millennials, born between 1980 and 2000 are browsers rather than buyers. The report found they create wishlists, both to engage with brands and for fun, with no intention of actually buying. Sometimes they don't have the money to make the purchase but save the item anyway. There is even the suggestion that these fauxsumers get the same kick out of saving an item as they would if they had bought it.

What started with the Amazon wishlist now plays out across mobile phone apps and social networking sites like Pinterest, where users curate pinboards of items they like as though that were their main goal, rather than actually owning anything on them.

Curating your fantasy buys on Pinterest or Tumblr offers you the thrill of shopping without having to pay anything. This collection and display of products in social media sites has become a way of expressing one's tastes and projecting a 'personal brand'. Entering luxury stores virtually allows you to 'roam about' without having the feeling of insecurity that the products being displayed may be out of your reach.

However, the process of fauxsumerism is not limited to millennials. The Accenture study of 2013 conducted market research on the shopping behaviours of 6,000 consumers, including 1,707 millennials across eight countries. Although millennials are the first truly connected generation, the study found similarities between the way they shop and the way Baby Boomers (born from 1946–1964) and Generation X (1965–1979) shop. Across all three demographics, 41% said they preferred 'showrooming' – looking at the merchandise in a retail store and then looking for it online to find the lowest price.

Meeting new demands

The fauxsumer certainly poses a challenge for the companies trying to sell goods. If customers get the same thrill out of putting an item on a list as they do from actually spending money on it, there is an obvious consequence.

All is not lost for shops though, they just need to adapt. The Accenture study also found that although millennials value online channels when checking out reviews, ratings and prices, they still prefer to visit bricks-and-mortar stores where they can touch an item, smell it and pick it up.

The findings also challenged the myth that millennials are not loyal customers. In fact, they seek a personalised memorable experience where their purchase or interaction is valued and they expect to receive targeted offers and discounts via email or post in return for their custom. That said, it turns out that they 'like' a retailer's Facebook page more often with the goal of keeping abreast of offers and news than to express an actual attachment to the brand.

Retailers need to convert browsers into buyers and should think smart to make that happen. Bricks-and-mortar retailers should include mobile devices in their in-store experience. They might send real-time promotions to their customers' phones as they browse or let them pay with their phone. Millennials expect integrated, seamless shopping, be it online or in store.

If shopping has become a source of entertainment for millennials, retailers need to take advantage of that and show customers a good time when they buy.

A bigger problem to solve is how to keep up with social media habits. Technologies like Facebook, Twitter, Pinterest and Tumblr are constantly evolving and users are moving around more than ever so retailers need to work out which is the best platform to use if they want to converse with customers, and adapt their strategies accordingly.

⇨ The above information is reprinted with kind permission from The Conversation. Please visit www.theconversation.com for further information.

*© 2010-2014,
The Conversation Trust (UK)*

Key facts

⇨ Mintel's research finds that...48% of consumers agree that "price matters more than whether a product is British" and 30% say "I do not feel any loyalty to buying British food and drink". (page 1)

⇨ 66% of UK consumers use a loyalty card. (page 2)

⇨ Women will spend a whopping £3,050.32 on high street shopping trips across the course of one year, compared to spends of just £611.43 for men. (page 4)

⇨ The average shopping trip for women lasts four hours. The average shopping trip for men lasts for one hour and 45 minutes. (page 4)

⇨ E-commerce is the fastest growing retail market in Europe, with sales in the UK, Germany, France, Sweden, The Netherlands, Italy, Poland and Spain expected to reach a combined total of £111.2 billion in 2014. (page 5)

⇨ In 2014 we expect online retail sales made via mobiles to grow in the UK by 62% to a total of £7.92 billion. This is equivalent to 17.6% of UK online retail sales. Sales using tablets will grow by 100% (to £3.10 billion) and smartphone retailing is expected to grow by 44.3% to £4.82 billion. Smartphones will still provide 60.8% of UK mobile shopping. (page 6)

⇨ ONS figures out last week found that 74% of all British adults have bought goods or services online. (page 7)

⇨ Today some 16% of all non-food retail happens online and how quickly the goods can be delivered is critical in consumers' buying decisions. (page 8)

⇨ 79% of consumers have viewed or shared content from a company's social media page. Younger browsers are most receptive to this particular form of advertising; the study finding that 21% of males aged 18–34 have bought a product straight after interacting with an ad on the likes of Facebook and Twitter. (page 8)

⇨ When you see items on a supermarket shelf, you are actually looking at a planogram. A planogram is defined as a 'diagram or model that indicates the placement of retail products on shelves in order to maximise sales'. (page 9)

⇨ Sweden, Norway and Quebec completely bar marketing to children under the age of 12. (page 13)

⇨ In 2013, the UK brand with the most positive brand among consumers during the last 12 months was BBC iPlayer. (page 16)

⇨ Your right to cancel an order starts the moment you place your order and ends 14 days from the day you receive it. (page 17)

⇨ Your right to cancel a service starts the moment you enter into the contract and lasts 14 days. (page 17)

⇨ You should get a refund within 14 days of either the trader getting the goods back, or you providing evidence of having returned the goods (for example, a proof of postage receipt from the post office), whichever is the sooner. (page 17)

⇨ It's illegal for a business to display any notice that deliberately misleads consumers or deceives them about their rights, e.g. a sign that says they don't accept returns or offer refunds. (page 20)

⇨ Traders operating hotlines for consumer complaints or questions, will not be able to charge more than the basic rate for such calls. (page 22)

⇨ Financial services firms can only operate in the UK if they are authorised by us or registered to do so, or are otherwise exempt. (page 24)

⇨ Sunday trading restrictions allow stores over 3,000 sq ft to open for six hours on a Sunday. But more than half of consumers (51%) believe further relaxation of the laws would benefit high streets as they emerge from the downturn. And just under half (48%) think large shops such as supermarkets should be allowed to open longer on Sundays. (page 26)

⇨ Half (49%) of UK adults aged 16 or over believe that, in general, retail companies are 'not very' or 'not at all' ethical nowadays ('ethical' is defined as selling products that are ethically produced and following good principles in their behaviour and decisions). (page 28)

⇨ Just under two in five (38%) agree that they try to buy products from companies that act in an ethical way, even if it means spending more, while one in five (22%) disagree. (page 29)

⇨ 62% agree that it is important that retail companies are clear about where they source their raw materials, components or ingredients from. (page 29)

⇨ Latest figures show that sales of ethical products grew by more than 12% in a year when the UK economy grew by only 0.2%. The ethical market is now worth just over £54 billion – greater than the market for alcohol and tobacco. (page 30)

⇨ Turning shops into showrooms for the Internet is an unsurprising consequence of straitened times, and 25 per cent of consumers did it in the run up to Christmas. (page 35)

Advergames

A method companies use to promote their organisation/ brand. A brand, product or message is woven into the game, which causes a lot of controversy, especially when the game is aimed at children.

Advertising

Advertising is communication between sellers and potential buyers. This can be delivered by various media, including radio, television, magazines, newspapers, billboards and website banners.

Consumer

A consumer is anyone who purchases and uses goods and services.

Consumer rights

A consumer has the right to expect certain standards in the goods they buy. The law says that the goods must be of satisfactory quality, fit for their purpose and as described. These statutory rights cover all goods bought or hired from a trader, including goods bought in sales.

Credit

A consumer can obtain goods and services before payment, based on an agreement that payment will be made at some point in the future. Other conditions may also be imposed. Forms of credit can include personal loans, overdrafts, credit cards, store cards, interest-free credit and hire purchase. However, reliance on credit can result in high levels of consumer debt.

E-commerce

Electronic business transactions, usually occurring via the Internet, e.g. purchasing goods online.

Economy

The way in which a region manages its resources. References to the 'national economy' indicate the financial situation of a country: how wealthy or prosperous it is.

Ethical consumerism

Buying things that are produced ethically – typically, things which do not involve harm to or exploitation of humans, animals or the environment; and also by refusing to buy products or services not made under these principles.

Expenditure

The act of paying out money.

Fair trade

Fair trade is about improving the income that goes to farm workers at the beginning of a supply chain, ensuring that they are paid a fair and stable price for the product supplied. Items produced using fair trade can be identified by the Fairtrade mark.

Fraud

The act of deceiving or conning someone for financial gain.

Gross Domestic Product (GDP)

The total value of the goods and services produced in a country within a year. This figure is used as a measure of a country's economic performance.

Interest

A fee charged on borrowed money. It is usually calculated as a percentage of the sum borrowed and paid in regular instalments. An 'interest rate' refers to the amount of money charged on a borrowed amount over a given period. Interest can also be earned on money which is deposited in a bank account and is paid regularly by the bank to the account holder.

Recession

A period during which economic activity has slowed, causing a reduction in Gross Domestic Product (GDP), employment, household incomes and business profits. If GDP shows a reduction over at least six months, a country is then said to be in recession. Recessions are caused by people spending less, businesses making less and banks being more reluctant to loan people money.

Scam

A scam is a scheme designed to trick consumers out of their money. Scams can take many forms, and are increasingly perpetrated over the Internet: 'phishing' scams, where a web user is sent an email claiming to be from their bank in order to gain access to their account, are one common example.

Assignments

Brainstorming

⇨ In small groups, discuss what you know about consumerism. Consider the following points:

- What is consumerism?
- What is a 'brand'?
- What do we mean by 'ethical consumerism'?
- What does the term 'materialistic' mean and how does this relate to consumerism?
- What is a consumer contract?

Research

⇨ Using the questions from the Mintel graph on page 1, plus some of your own, conduct some research amongst your friends and family to find out what matters more when making a purchasing decision: brand, price or quality. Write a report to analyse your findings and include at least three graphs or infographics.

⇨ Conduct a questionnaire amongst your class to find out how much people spend when they go shopping. You should compare and contrast the differences between males and females, and ask people about their online shopping habits as well as when they physically visited the shops. Write a report to analyse your findings and include at least three graphs or infographics.

⇨ In pairs, visit your local high street and count the number of shops that are vacant or closing down. Feedback to your class and discuss why you think high streets are changing.

⇨ Choose a brand that you are familiar with and research the techniques they use to encourage people to buy their products/services. For example, advertising campaigns, tie-ins with films or TV sponsorship, etc. Write a short paragraph summarising your findings.

Design

⇨ Design a poster that will encourage people to make ethical purchasing decisions.

⇨ Choose one of the articles in this book and create an illustration to highlight the key themes/message of your chosen article.

⇨ Design an app that will change the way people shop. It could be something that helps them compare prices, an app that tells you when you are near shops that might interest you or perhaps something that will help you find ethical alternatives for what you want to buy. Get creative and include sketches to illustrate your ideas!

⇨ Choose a brand or product and design a promotional 'advergame' aimed at their target audience.

Oral

⇨ 'Sunday trading laws should be relaxed, they are antiquated and no longer appropriate for our society.' Debate this motion as a class, with one group arguing in favour and the other against.

⇨ In pairs, discuss the tricks that supermarkets use to encourage people to spend more money. List as many different promotional methods as you can think of, then discuss with the rest of your class.

⇨ Create a simple leaflet that explains your consumer rights when buying products. You should include information about digital content purchases.

⇨ In pairs, role-play a situation in which one of you is trying to convince the other to become less materialistic. Think carefully about what you will say to validate your argument.

⇨ Ask a relative who is older than you how they think consumerism has changed in the last ten years. Write some notes and feedback to your class.

Reading/writing

⇨ Write a blog post about the rise of e-commerce. Include some ideas about where you think digital retail might go in the future.

⇨ Write a one-paragraph definition of ethical retail.

⇨ Read the article *Online retailing: Britain, Europe and the US 2014* on page 5 and write a summary for your school newspaper.

⇨ Watch the Morgan Spurlock documentary film *Supersize Me* and write a review exploring how the director deals with the theme of brand awareness.

⇨ Imagine you work for a charity that promotes ethical consumerism. Plan a social media campaign that will encourage people to change their shopping habits.

⇨ Write a letter to your local MP explaining why you think there should be more stringent rules surrounding the issue of advertising to children.

⇨ Read the article *Hard-to-please 'fauxsumers' pin it and save it but rarely buy it* on page 39 and write a blog post from the point of view of a 'fauxsumer', exploring the joys of being able to 'pin' products or add them to your shopping basket without actually going through to purchase them.

advergames, food industry 14
advertising
   to children 12–13, 14
   financial services 25
   and social media 8

banking, ethical 34
boycotts 34
BrandIndex Rankings 16
Brazilian products 2

call charges, consumer rights 19
cancellation rights 17–18, 22–3
children
   and food advertising 12–13
   and food industry online games 14
   impact of consumer culture 15–16
cloud-based software, consumer rights 23
Consumer Contracts Regulations 17–19
consumer culture, impact on children 15–16
consumer rights 17–27
Consumer Rights Directive, EU 22–3
consumer trends, UK 1–3
consumers
   brand awareness 16
   ethical shopping 28–33
   influence of social media 8
cooperatives 34
cultural influences and consumer trends 1

dark stores 35
data monitoring 2–3
delivery
   consumer rights 18–19
   and online retailing 8
   same-day 11–12
digital products, consumer rights 18, 23
distance selling, consumer rights 20, 21
   see also online shopping
drinks, healthy 3
Duchy Originals 31

e-books, consumer rights 23
e-commerce *see* online shopping
eco-travel 31, 34
electricity, green 34
energy drinks, healthy 3
ethical retail
   consumer behaviour 30–31

ethical shopping tips 34
   public opinions 28–9
   supply chain transparency 32–3
EU Consumer Rights Directive 22–3
Europe, online retailing 5

facings 9–10
Fairphone 33
Fairtrade 31
false consumerism 39
faulty goods, consumer rights 19
fauxsumers 39
financial services firms 24–5
food industry
   advergames 14
   advertising to children 12–13
   ethical products 30–31

foreign influences and consumer trends 1

gender
   and ethical shopping 28–9
   and shopping trips 4–5
green energy 31, 34
green home products 31

healthy drinks 3
healthy food, advertising to children 12–13
helpline charges, consumer rights 19
high street, future of 35–8
home products, ethical 31

information
   consumer rights 17
   supply chain transparency 32–3
internationalism and consumer trends 1

m-commerce *see* mobile shopping
market development, online retailing 6
marketing strategies
   supermarkets 9–10
   see also advertising
men
   ethical shopping 28, 29
   shopping trips 4, 5

mobile shopping 6, 7

MP3 players, consumer rights 23

national provenance of products 1

number of facings 9–10

nutritional analysis services 3

online shopping 5–8

   consumer rights 20, 21

   fantasy shopping 39

   and the high street 35–6

overseas selling 21

personal products, ethical 31

planograms 9–10

privacy issues 2–3

refunds 17–18, 20, 22–3

repair and replacement 20

returning goods 19, 20

Sale of Goods Act 21

same-day delivery 11–12

self-analysis 2–3

self-esteem and consumer culture 15–16

services, cancellation rights 18

shelving strategies, supermarkets 9–10

shopping

   future of 35–8

shopping trips 4–5

   see also ethical retail; online shopping

showrooming 35

social media

   and fantasy shopping 39

   influence on consumers 8

software, cloud-based, consumer rights 23

stores

   impact of online shopping 6, 7

   impact of same-day delivery 11–12

Subway, marketing to children 12

Sunday trading 26–7

supermarkets

   marketing strategies 9–10

   and Sunday trading 26–7

supply chain transparency 32–3

sweet manufacturers, advergames 14

technology use in stores 38

transparency 32–3

transport, ethical 31, 34

US, online retailing 5–6

wearable technology 3

well-being of children, impact of consumer culture 15–16

women

   ethical shopping 28, 29

   shopping trips 4–5

Acknowledgements

The publisher is grateful for permission to reproduce the material in this book. While every care has been taken to trace and acknowledge copyright, the publisher tenders its apology for any accidental infringement or where copyright has proved untraceable. The publisher would be pleased to come to a suitable arrangement in any such case with the rightful owner.

Images

All images courtesy of iStock, except page 22: Wikimedia.Icons used on pages 2, 29, 33 © Freepik. Money icon on page 2 © Icons8. Magnifying glass icon on pages 2 and 41 © SimpleIcon.

Illustrations

Don Hatcher: pages 11 & 34. Simon Kneebone: pages 13 & 36. Angelo Madrid: pages 7 & 20.

Additional acknowledgements

Editorial on behalf of Independence Educational Publishers by Cara Acred.

With thanks to the Independence team: Mary Chapman, Sandra Dennis, Christina Hughes, Jackie Staines and Jan Sunderland.

Cara Acred

Cambridge

January 2015